UNPUNISHED

How to Let Go of Punishments and Find Your Parenting Peace

Michelle Kenney M.Ed.

MK Publishing

WHAT THEY'RE SAYING...

"Michelle has created an incredible, empowering guide to parenting in a way that builds a deeper connection with your children and teens. Through her own vulnerability, she shares how to take ego out of parenting. *UnPunished* provides parenting tools that work and offers suggestions for how to get back on track during those inevitable times of struggle."

– Alyce Chan, Comedian and Founder of @MOMCOM-NYC

"*UnPunished* is the handbook every parent needs if they want to build a deeper connection with their kids and bring peace back into their homes. I wish I had a copy to refer to during these formative years!"

– Cynthia Muchnick, MA, Co-Author of *The Parent Compass*, Educational Consultant, Speaker www.cynthiamuchnick.com

"Connection is the cornerstone of creating harmonious, healthy, and happy relationships between parents and children. In *UnPunished*, Michelle lays out an effective path to achieving peaceful parenting, and reveals her own journey to this discovery with keen insight, humor, and vulnerability."

– Dr. Jessica Zucker, Author of *I Had a Miscarriage: A Memoir, a Movement.*

"Michelle does an excellent job breaking down perfectionism and its downsides in this read. Great for getting perspective for parents looking to raise kids with good values but also adequately prepare them for the world."

- Julian Sarafian, Lawyer, Mental Health Advocate

"Michelle shows her readers a way to parent without relying on bribes, threats, and manipulations. It's *UnPunished*! We don't want to shame and guilt children for how they feel. We want to help them build their confidence. In her book, Michelle shares how to train, teach, model and encourage rather than force and control, so that parents can create a more positive developmental experience for children. Like Michelle, I too am a huge believer in parenting without punishments."

– Dr. Siggie Cohen, Child Development Specialist

"If you're wanting to shift from punishment to peace and control to connection in your parenting, *UnPunished* is for you! Michelle shares her wisdom with empathy and encouragement as someone who knows the struggle firsthand and can guide you in creating a more peaceful, compassionate relationship with your child. "

– Iris Chen, author of *Untigering*

UNPUNISHED: How to Let Go of Punishments and Find Your Parenting Peace

By Michelle Kenney, M.Ed.

ISBN: 978-0-578-28158-2 (print only)

Design and Editing Support by www.bookformulapublishing.com

MK Publishing, Los Angeles, CA For more information,
email michelle@peaceandparentingla.com.

Limit of Liability/Disclaimer of Warranty: This publication is designed to provide accurate and authoritative information in regard to the subject matter covered. It is for informational purposes only and not meant to replace the advice of a licensed professional.

It is sold with the understanding that neither the author nor the publisher is engaged in rendering medical advice or other professional services. While the publisher and author have used their best efforts in preparing this book, they make no representations or warranties regarding the information provided.

You should consult with a professional where appropriate. Neither the publisher nor the author shall be liable for any loss or damages, including but not limited to special, incidental, consequential, personal, or other damages.

UNHINGED: How to Let Go of Pandemonium and Find Your Friendly Place

By Michelle Kenney, M.Ed.

ISBN: 978-0-578-28158-2 (print only)

Design and Editing Support by www.[illegible]publishing.com

MK Publishing, [illegible], CA. For more information:
email: [illegible]

Contents

Get Your Free Gift!

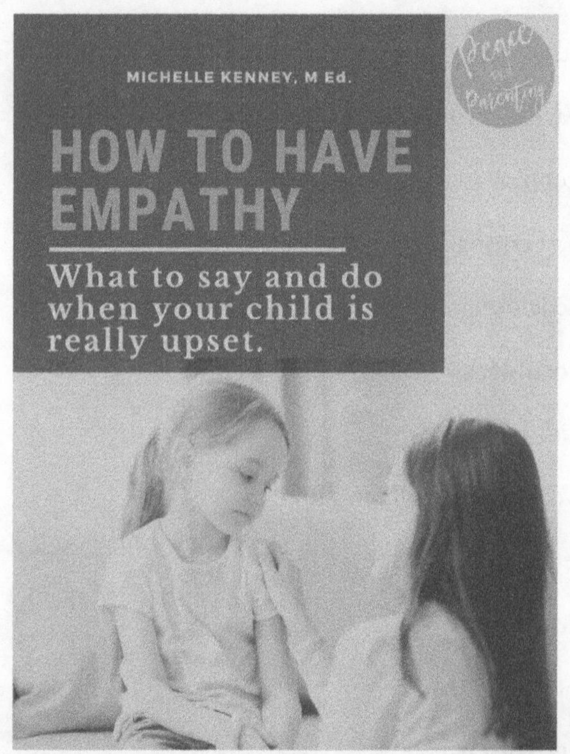

HOW TO HAVE EMPATHY

To get the best experience with this book, I encourage readers to download and read *Connection 101: How to Get and Stay Connected to Your Child Every Day.* This primer will help you implement what you've learned faster and take the next steps needed to reach your parenting goals.

You can get a copy by visiting:
https://courses.peaceandparentingla.com/empathy
http://courses.Peaceandparentingla.com/connection101

For Esme and Pia

(my heart and soul)

Foreword

In the work of parenting, we parents face a steep learning curve. From the day our first child is born until the day our last child leaves to explore the world on their own, we must navigate situations we've never faced before or faced many times with unsatisfying results. It's not easy to find our way, although we have so much love to bring to our children. One of the ways we learn best is by hearing the stories of other parents.

Unpunished is full of such stories. And more. It's replete with stories told with honesty and humility, and each story unfolds to reveal fresh insights and hard-won wisdom. The frame is the author's struggle with perfectionism, but there's much more here: thoughts about control and connection, becoming attuned to each of your children, resolving sibling tensions, handling the expectations of others, real and imagined, and what self-care for parents might entail.

Michelle Kenney is straightforward, kind, and mindful of parents' efforts and dedication. You will not feel judged. No unattainable standards are put before you. No casual advice is tossed about. And one of the blessings of *Unpunished* is its brevity. There's much to enjoy and to think about, but not at the expense of too much of your precious time. You'll feel like you've had a nourishing visit with a best friend you haven't yet met, leaving you with ideas to ponder and experiments to try.

Unpunished is a book that comes from the heart, and from the point of view that we parents do our very best, every day, even when we're at our wits' end. The compassion and richly positive perspective that follows will refresh your spirits and sustain your efforts like a cool glass of water on a hot day. Michelle Kenney's journey in parenting—her stories, her unfolding wisdom, and her hard-won understanding of the challenges of parenting—await you. A kinder, more generous guide would be hard to find!

Patty Wipfler
Founder/ Hand in Hand Parenting

Introduction

What is a perfect parent?

Before the realities of parenting wrapped around my ankles and dragged me kicking and screaming through the mud, I thought I had it all figured out. I'd created this full visual in my mind of what the "perfect" mom would look like and how she would behave. Just like a child envisioning her future as a doctor or owning her own company, I could see this woman vividly in my mind, and I longed to be her. For me, perfection was tangible, if I could just become the woman I'd imagined. Everyone has their own idea of what perfect parenting looks like. For me, it was all about being hands-on and engaged in every aspect of my child's life. The ideal mom would insist on breastfeeding her children until they were two. She'd forgo medication, make organic baby food and keep her little ones away from sugar and electronics. She'd be an active parent in school and make sure her kids were involved in every activity. This same mom would go to all the school events, be the room mom, and be in charge of fundraising. Playdates and birthday parties would be elaborate affairs, and life would revolve around her children.

Somewhere in the back of my mind, I saw attached parenting as the key to parenting success and that being my child's best friend would equal a relationship free of conflict. If I was attuned and present for my children on every level, I believed that we'd never fight or struggle. It just made sense to me. If I were everything to my child, there wouldn't be room for friction.

Looking back, I am now acutely aware of the crazy amount of pressure I placed on myself to achieve some hollowed-out version of perfection. On the surface, being in control allowed me to forget the shame of my childhood that was simmering just under the surface. Unfortunately, the monster that I created in my mind would become the pseudo-identity that I gladly linked arms with well beyond my 20s. Even when I questioned the health and stability of my own upbringing, seeking perfection continued to feel "safe". I felt empowered and in control, even when the foundation of everything I thought I knew was crumbling beneath me.

Coming to a place where I could acknowledge the unseen cracks in my exterior didn't happen overnight. Even after years of deep dives and intensive therapy, I still couldn't shake the vision of perfection that had embedded itself into my core. I needed to be her. She was my "fix", that habit that drove me to make poor choices and hurt those I loved.

Not What I Expected

Coming into motherhood was like entering the fourth quarter of a football game as a rookie quarterback with only a playbook and no previous playing time. I was completely lambasted by the front line and fumbled the ball almost immediately. I found myself at the bottom of a dog pile and the ball was nowhere to be seen. Defeat swept in immediately, and I could taste the blood in my mouth. I struggled to play the game and continued to get sacked over and over again. I didn't want to be in this place, but I couldn't seem to dig my way out.

As the need for perfection continued to scrape away my self-worth, I would place it on an even higher pedestal. If I could somehow reach that ideal pinnacle, then that would prove that I was a good parent, make that a great parent. In my heart, I believed that reaching my vision of perfection was the only way to be truly happy.

What I failed to see in the "perfect" mom narrative was that a) she was unattainable, and b) despite her desire to create the "perfect" family with her perfectionism, she would only continue to disappoint herself when she didn't live up to that impossible standard. I thought that if I could just learn enough about being a parent, then I would be prepared for anything, so I read all the books on attachment parenting. I wanted to be *that* parent, the one who responded to all of my baby's needs—breastfed on demand, co-slept, and was always there for my baby every waking moment.

Despite my best efforts (I tried so hard!), it just didn't work. As a parent of one child and then two, I couldn't keep up the frenetic pace because mental, physical, and emotional exhaustion always outran me. Wanting to pull my hair out was a real thing, and calling my husband every day at 5 pm to tell him I was running away was not an idle threat. I really couldn't take being with our kids one more minute.

It wasn't until a friend from school suggested that I look into Hand in Hand Parenting that things shifted. Through their teaching, I learned to apply connective parenting to raising my girls and finally felt a sense of normalcy. I'd like to say that the rest was history, but the reality is that my world flipped inside out and then upside down before things finally settled. Despite the upheaval, I can honestly say that what began as a rescue mission over time turned into a transformative journey of love, connection, and hope.

Connective parenting became my lifeline—a proven method for transforming how I parented that I could finally trust. That unrealistic commitment I had to perfect parenting slowly transformed into an enriching and life-altering parenting experience. It has forever changed how I see my beautiful daughters and given me the courage to embrace myself—flaws and all—through their eyes.

It's not working!

I get it, and I've been there. When you put all of your effort into parenting and nothing seems to work, it can be heartbreaking. If we, the parents, can't get it right, what does that mean for our children? It's so easy to question ourselves and wonder why things aren't working out. What are we *not* doing? How is it possible that we messed up something that should have come naturally?

Trust me, I asked myself the same questions over and over again as I continued trying to force them into my "perfect" box that didn't fit. I was the parent, and they were the child, so why weren't things working?

Parenting struggles look different for everyone. While I struggled with perfection and keeping up appearances, maybe you parent from a place of fear—fear of failure, so you push too hard.

Maybe you feel overworked and tired, so you're resentful, unenthusiastic, and less likely to set limits, or you're on the opposite end of the spectrum and helicopter parent by hovering and over-lecturing. Or, perhaps you struggle with physical punishments and find yourself spanking, yanking, or grabbing your child to get them to obey.

Whatever your challenge, what we all have in common is that it hurts when we don't connect with our children. They're a part of us, so we feel their pain, even when the way they express that pain makes us uncomfortable.

The reason connective parenting works is that it's built on unconditional acceptance—not the back-and-forth games that we play when we're trying to get our children to comply. It encourages empathy over yelling, bribery, and punishment and doesn't define behavior as good or bad, but uses it as an indicator of what the child truly needs.

It's Not What You Think

Have you ever wondered why child behavior "fixes" lose steam over time? It's because most of them embrace conformity and the idea that if we forcibly place our child into a set of parameters, then eventually they will comply. Think of punishments like yelling, taking away privileges, grounding, and timeouts that are dished out to control how our children behave.

While these may work in the short term because they work off of fear, control, and intimidation, eventually, children figure it out and learn to leverage their own "power" to get what they want from us.

Have you noticed that the more you punish, the more your kids seem to "test the waters"? If punishments worked, then wouldn't the "bad" behavior have stopped after the first time? Do we think that our kids just don't have good memories? Of course they do. Their memories are often better than ours.

It's the same with punishments because our kids learn how to adapt over time. They become adept at weighing their behavior against perceived outcomes and then making a choice. Whether they misbehave to get more attention or choose the risk of punishment in favor of the perceived reward, many kids take control from us by becoming masters of the game. The same control we try to exert over them to change their behavior is met by an equal willingness on their part to control their environment at all costs.

Parent First

I am a parent first and a coach second. I have been where you are and continue to struggle from time to time, but unlike the beginning of my parenting journey, I now understand that there's no such thing as perfect parenting. When I adopted connective parenting as a lifestyle, I finally found something that worked.

In the pages of this book, I am going to show you how to push the reset button on parenting by giving you a new way to think about how we engage with our child(ren). This is not a "quick fix" or a magic system of parenting that will suddenly bring everything into balance, but it is a process that you can follow and build upon consistently to restore trust, respect, and deep connection with your children.

By taking an inside-out approach, parenting becomes more organic and leads to the following benefits:

- Accountability
- Respect for others
- Self-Confidence
- Self-Regulation

- Self-Healing
- Cooperation
- Strong parent-child connection

Parenting doesn't come with a parachute, but without a plan in place, everything you do will be a hit or a miss. The connective parenting approach changed all of that for me, and I am so excited to share my experiences with you.

If you are tired, frustrated, losing patience, discouraged, feeling defeated, and struggling with guilt, *or* if you're out of options, have given up on punishments, are feeling disrespected, and at your wit's end, welcome to real-life parenting. The good news is that even if you've tried everything and failed, there's still another way.

We all need a "do-over" from time to time and trust me, parenting comes with a lot of potholes. If we don't know what to look for, it's easy to fall in and get stuck.

This book is for any parent who has come to the end of their rope and realized there's still a long way to the bottom. If you've tried it "your way" and now find yourself questioning your sanity to ever think that you could do this parenting thing well, then you're going to want to hear what I have to say. There is light at the end of the long parenting tunnel, and I'm here to help you find it.

This book is my journey from hopelessness and discouragement to a life lived with accountability and purpose. I am honest about my struggles and share how I learned to parent strategically and without shame. This has come with a lot of trial and error, but I've learned to embrace my children as inherently great people who want to do the right thing. All they need is an unencumbered opportunity to figure things out in a space where they feel safe.

I want you to come away from this book with less stress and anxiety over getting everything right. There's no such thing as perfect parenting. All we can do is give our best and continue to evolve as we gain the skills and insight needed to make better choices.

There are still days when I do or say the wrong things, but I try to forgive myself because I finally understand that "perfection" is not the ultimate goal. When I mess up now, I forgive myself, move on, and do the same with my children.

This book and all its anecdotes are just about the process, the difficult unwinding of my own shame, my own control, and my perfectionism. I hope something I say gives you some comfort.

The journey is not easy and can take lots of time and effort, but it is so worth it, and parenting with more love and connection will never steer you wrong. I promise you.

I have tried and failed at parenting more times than I can count, but I have also had tremendous wins, which have made all that I've been through worth the effort. Although I am now a certified parenting coach, it didn't start that way, and that's the part I want to share with you in the pages of this book.

No matter how many degrees or certifications are tacked on to the end of my name, I will never consider myself an "expert" when it comes to parenting because it's a lifelong journey. It is my sincerest hope that you'll see a part of yourself in my story and know that you can make it out of the hole, too.

This book is for parents who are ready to invest time and effort into supporting their child's development on a deeper level. They are willing to take the necessary steps to uncover any of their own psychological, emotional, or physical scars that are seeping into their parenting and do the deeper work to uproot any behaviors that are counterproductive to seeing positive results.

If you are looking for a bandaid to just make the "bad" behavior stop, then this book is NOT for you. While it's common to experience some quick "wins" with connective parenting, the solutions I suggest require a long-term commitment and adherence to the process.

On the surface, connective parenting can feel like you're giving away your "power" as a parent, but if you stick with me, I'll show you how to use connective parenting in a way that empowers both you and your child.

At the publishing of this book, I have two teenagers—Esme and Pia. At times, they've been my unknowing guinea pigs through the learning process, and I've been theirs. It's taken years to find a place of balance, but even that shifts from time to time because the parent-child relationship is ever-evolving. It's a continual process of re-evaluating where we are and where we're going because our children are always changing, and so are we.

I hope this book will shatter the parenting myths that lock so many of us into the suffocating cycle of "perfect parenting". After going through the heart-wrenching pain of parenting without a parachute and then hitting rock bottom, I am so grateful that I found a better way.

I believe with all of my heart that if you give connective parenting a chance, then you will see amazing results. I've seen parents, families, and children's lives transformed through the process, so I have complete confidence that it will work for you as well.

Don't sit on this one. Peaceful parenting is a real thing. It's just waiting for you to take the first step.

—Michelle

1

My Road to Empathy

“People are too complicated to have simple labels.” - Philip Pullman, *The Amber Spyglass*

Every morning would begin the same. Like an alcoholic who promises herself that she won’t drink, I would tell myself that regardless of what came my way that day, I would remain calm and refrain from yelling. I so desperately wanted to be the mother I imagined—in tune with my child, not letting upsets get to me—but I just couldn’t do it.

Looking back now, I realize I just wanted to have control. If I could get everyone to do things my way without pushback or disruptions, then everything would be fine. In the early days of my parenting journey, it was all about my comfort and staying as far away from discomfort as possible regardless of how it affected those around me.

But this is not how a household with two young children works, and I can't imagine why I thought otherwise, but I did. Every time my kids' feelings erupted or they behaved in a way that I thought was inappropriate, it felt like a personal attack on me which left me in a constant emotional state of emergency.

I remember one morning when my daughter Esme was in kindergarten. Getting ready for school had become a nightmare because she refused to get dressed. She'd try on a bunch of outfits only to take them off and then throw them on the floor, complaining that they were uncomfortable and itchy. This particular morning was no different, and as usual, I didn't handle it very well.

I sat there on the dark brown plush carpet in her room and watched the scene unfold. I remember looking around and thinking about how normal the day looked. Warm sunlight streamed through her window and everything seemed so bright and alive, but, what was playing out in front of me, was anything but joyful. I was miserable, and so was Esme. It was like a bad dream that kept looping each day, and I couldn't escape.

From her pink walls and big-girl bed to her fluffy white covers and huge stuffed pink bear in the corner, I knew the scene well. The perfect stage was set, but the star of the show,

Esme, was on strike. She was messing up all of her lines and not following any of my cues.

I handled my daughter's emotions like I was the director of a major motion picture that was about to be shut down if I didn't get everything back on track.

In my mind our mission was clear. We had to go to school, be on time, and not let anything get in our way. *I would not be late! I needed others to see me as a good mom, and good moms were punctual, and their children were always well-behaved and prepared. This was my only focus, and I would achieve it at all costs.*

Back then, shame was my biggest motivator. I couldn't bear the thought of a teacher or parent thinking that I didn't have it all together. The threat of shame followed me everywhere, and it didn't take much for it to show up and cover me like a prickly, winter blanket.

This meant that my choice to get Esme ready by any means necessary guaranteed an emotional roller coaster ride every morning, but if that's what it took for me to save face in front of onlookers, then I was willing to do it.

So, this "production" of getting Esme dressed in the morning, *my show*, was all about having every box checked for me and my kids. I had my strategy down to a science.

First, I would threaten. Then I would yell, and finally, I would try to scare her into doing what I said. By the time she was dressed, everyone was an emotional wreck. With tears streaming down her face and me feeling like a tight rubber band about to snap, we'd walk out that door with her little sister in tow—three sad and angry humans making a trek to school while wiping tears.

As I passed other families and tried to pretend like we were happy, I remember asking myself: *Is this how it's supposed to work? Do other families go through this every morning just to get ready for school? Are we normal?*

I finally came to the conclusion that what we were doing wasn't normal, but not because I accepted any responsibility or that there could be something deeper going on with me. Instead, I blamed the problem on Esme and convinced myself that something had to be going on with her. She simply needed a diagnosis, so we could fix the issue.

I began researching any disorders that fit her behavior. After making my own assessment, I stuffed all of her "uncomfortable behaviors" into a neat little box, labeled her broken, and settled on her needing an Occupational Therapist. What I thought would be the solution to all of our problems was just the beginning.

A Journey to Realization

So, we started therapy. Weekly, Esme and I would walk into a large, imposing, industrial office building deep in the San Fernando Valley in Los Angeles, where we'd take the elevator to the top floor to her therapy session. While there, kind young therapists would take Esme through her play activities in their indoor gym. I felt proactive. I was doing what any good parent would do, getting to the root of Esme's "problem" so that our family would be okay.

After the therapists took her through fun obstacle courses and let her put her hands in sticky goo, they told us she had tactile defensiveness disorder, which meant that she had a processing issue. They recommended a brushing protocol, and I felt ecstatic. We'd finally found the solution!

Relief swept over me. Everything I'd bottled up, the worry and frustration, finally had a place to go. Her diagnosis confirmed that it wasn't me and that it was her. I knew something was wrong, and this proved it. Now it made sense why things had been so hard. I could almost hang my hat on the idea that everything stemmed from this "disorder".

After her diagnosis, we started the recommended protocol which required weekly "therapy". We brushed her skin and did everything we were told to do, but we still struggled.

Even though there was no improvement, I was still blaming everything on her so-called "disorder." I blindly committed myself to get her better so things would be easier for all of us. "Better" for her meant *better* for us.

This went on for several months until I found Hand in Hand Parenting and learned about letting go of punishments and rewards. This new concept was so counterintuitive to what I knew that I had a hard time framing it in my mind. *No punishments? How does that work?* I'd been so deeply entrenched in the weeds of our crazy morning routine that my only thought was how we could get ready for school if I didn't threaten or bribe.

Regardless of my reservations, something was compelling about not having to twist and manipulate our interactions to have some sense of normalcy in our days. I was desperate and willing to try anything. The brushing protocol was not working. I needed something new.

It took a few weeks, but I finally began to let go of control parenting, manipulations, and threats. Guess who started to wear her clothes? Guess who began to get ready for school without a fuss? Guess who said: Mommy, I like the new mommy so much better than the old, mean mommy? Guess whose heart broke into a million pieces?

The Conformist

As I shared, early in my parenting, I blamed Esme for all of our difficulties. I demonized her by letting her take the responsibility for all that was wrong instead of looking inwardly at myself.

Why?

Well, one because if someone didn't take the blame, then I would have to and two, because my youngest daughter Pia was doing just fine. She wasn't asserting herself in unmanageable ways and causing me to second-guess my parenting. To me, that said it all. I was a "good" mom because Pia was proof that I was doing my job. Or was she?

Every child wants to know that they are seen, heard, and loved unconditionally.

Pia came into this world full of soul, maturity, and great comedic timing. What she wasn't was difficult. She had an "easy-going" temperament that made it effortless to parent her. I could threaten or bribe her right into place where I needed her. This is why it was so easy for me to make Esme the fall guy for all that went wrong. Pia didn't push back or get angry with me, and when she misbehaved even slightly, which was rare, I would swiftly send her to a little time out and all was better.

Pia was the one that was "right" and good—what my friends and I would call *easy.* "She's my easy child", I would remark with a knowing smile. She was proof that I was doing something right in my parenting. Her "good" behavior crowned me as a "good" mom, which was the coveted blue ribbon from the society that I craved. She was the perfect complement to the ideal mom fantasy I envisioned.

In my mind, if others thought I did my job as a parent well, then they wouldn't judge me. I wouldn't have to endure the shame of not being good enough. Their approval would give me validation and self-worth. With Pia, I felt like I belonged in that club.

The only problem was that I couldn't ignore what was going on with Esme. It was right there in my face, every day, reminding me that something was off. As much as I wanted to blame her for our disconnect, I knew deep down that something else might be going on, and soon I'd discover that what I thought was "compliant" behavior in Pia was just her stuffing her feelings.

The reality was that my relationship with Pia was just as stressed as the one I shared with Esme. With both of them, I'd always focused on changing their behavior instead of connecting with them on a deeper level. I only wanted their obedience because, in my mind, that was the gold standard of good parenting. Pia felt disconnected, just like her sister. She just responded differently.

Words can't describe how shocked I was when I found out just how badly my sweet Pia was feeling inside.

Playing with Dolls

Raising kids in Los Angeles can be interesting, especially if, like me, you were raised in a small town like Medford, Oregon.

One summer, when Pia was around four, I took her to The Grove, an outdoor mall in Los Angeles.

Pia and I were on a Special Time date because I'd recently started implementing our one-on-one time after a parenting coach recommended I try it. I was finally on a journey to better parenting and was just as excited as my little Pia was to share time together.

We rode the escalator down four stories and exited onto the palatial marble floor. It feels like Main Street at Disneyland, with cobblestone streets and a city clock. After making the prerequisite stops at the giant fountain, Wetzel Pretzel for a snack, and Pottery Barn Kids store, we finally made our way to Pia's *store of all stores*—The American Girl Doll store.

If you're not already familiar with the phenomenon that is the American Girl Doll store, consider yourself lucky. This two-story flagship store is stuffed with dolls of every shape, color, and size along with enough accessories and clothes to make your head spin. It is even equipped with a salon for dolls where you can make an appointment to have your doll's hair styled or ears pierced.

As we walked through my little girl's paradise, she touched every doll she could get her hands on. Her favorites, the Bitty Babies, were just her size with their "real" blinking eyes and soft, silky hair. We stayed for what I thought was forever, which admittedly was probably more like 20 minutes. Even a few seconds in that place gives me the hives.

Finally, it was time to go home. Esme was waiting, and we needed to get back so I could make dinner. When I told Pia we had to leave, she mildly resisted, which was unlike her, but coaxing her out of the Bitty Baby Room and onto the escalator wasn't difficult. If there was one thing Pia liked, it was a good escalator ride.

We descended to the second floor, and she immediately ran to the next moving staircase downward. When we got to the bottom, she begged me to let her go again. Of course, I said "yes", but with my serious voice I let her know it would be the last time because we needed to get home.

This time my sweet, compliant, and "easy" child... for the first time in her life, refused to comply. She looked me directly in the eyes and said, "No!"

I don't know if I was shocked or what, but I obliged and again we went up two flights and back down. It finally occurred to me that my sweet child was not going to leave. I'd recently stopped using threats and bribes, so there was nothing for me to rely on for compliance and Pia knew it.

Then she began to scream and yell.

I knew about listening to feelings at this point, and so I listened as I held her hand, but I needed to get home and my patience was wearing thin. As she wailed and fought and hit me in my shins, she tried to pull away from me so she could run. Halfway to the fountain, she yanked her hand away and sprinted from me as fast as her little tiny body would take her.

In her fit of anger, I don't think she realized she was running directly into the path of the trolley, which I could see out of the corner of my eye. It was rounding the bend at Anthropologie and heading directly for my sweet little girl.

I had no choice except to run as fast as I could and scoop her into my arms as she kicked, hit, and grabbed at me. She wanted to go back to the American Girl Doll Store and made sure everyone in the mall knew it.

If you know anything about LA, you know there are always lots of people everywhere. Standing there flushed, with a screaming child, in the center of an outdoor mall, I felt embarrassed and ashamed. I was sure that hundreds of people were watching me fail at mothering.

Pia didn't calm down, not in The Grove and not for over an hour. We eventually made it to my car where I sat in the back with her as she cried and screamed and told me just how awful I was.

I stayed calm, but I wasn't calm on the inside. It wasn't because I had a hard time sitting through tantrums. After Esme's multiple-hour tantrums, I knew the routine, but Pia's tantrum was different. It was big and hard and unearthing. In the end, she held me so tight.

As I sat in the car and watched Pia, I felt the pain of my hurting child and my own hurt from embarrassment and shame. I didn't understand what had just happened. All I saw were broken pieces. I was no longer a "good" mom. I'd failed. Society had just swallowed me up and spit me out. I was bad because I had a child who hit and kicked me, had tantrums, and screamed in public.

During that episode at The Grove, the false narrative that I'd created in my mind about being a "good" mom crumbled. My "easy" child had big feelings that were just beginning to surface. Why? Because I was paying attention.

I didn't understand it all, but I knew she needed me in this way. We'd stumbled upon a moment of genuine connection. Despite the momentary discomfort, I understood the importance of what had just happened. Pia needed the space to express her real feelings, and I wanted to be the one to give her that opportunity.

In retrospect, I can see everything from Pia's perspective. She'd seen me sit by Esme's side for months, guiding her through her upsets. Pia wanted her turn, too. In that special moment, she finally had the courage to release her true feelings.

The experience caused me to re-evaluate what "good" children were and if that was even a real thing. In the end, Pia was the most precious, golden human who showed me all the parts of her, not just the person she thought I wanted her to see so she could please me.

That day at The Grove, I won the prize of connection but simultaneously lost the golden ticket for being a "good mom". Why couldn't I reconcile the two?

The Disconnected Child

Early on, I mistook outbursts for negative behavior and conformity as good behavior, not realizing that both were two sides of the same disconnection coin. Every child has a unique way of responding to the world around them. It's up to us to read what they show us as well as what they don't, and then put it into the proper context.

Our society is quick to pull out the "bad child" card. It's easy to assess a situation from a distance and then jump to a conclusion without having all the details. It's important to consider questions like, "What really happened?" "Is my child acting out because they don't feel seen or heard?" "Is there a deeper story that I'm not seeing?" "Am I taking a balanced approach to my conclusion, or am I bringing my own baggage into the assessment?" "What is the root cause of this behavior?" "How can I remove my feelings from this situation and view it from a more holistic perspective?"

Severing Ties

Have you ever responded "Because I said so" when your child whined,

"But why?????????????"

When you've given every rational answer under the sun for your decision and your child still insists on questioning your reasoning, they are trying to get their needs met. They want an answer that eventually leads to a "yes."

Since you're the parent "Because I said so" feels like your ace in the hole, but power plays never win the war. Our children are resilient. They simply restrategize and come from another angle the next time.

A power play is anything used to gain leverage over someone else. From the parent's side, this could look like yelling or withholding affection or attention to induce fear. Yelling scares a child into submission while withholding affection or attention induces the fear of not receiving the basic necessities of a healthy relationship—love and consideration.

From the child's side, what can look like a power play on their part is often the manifestation of a child's disconnective state. All kids operate from a place of trying to get their needs met. This can show up as a tantrum, showing defiance, hitting their siblings, or asking you "but, why?" so many times that you finally give in.

When you set out to control your child's environment through power plays, you are creating an arena for future battles. Every act of control on our part sets up another wall in our child's enclosure, and they'll continue to push against it until they get the outcome that they want. This has to do with the latent development of their prefrontal cortex that is connected to their decision-making. An article by Raising Children offers a great description:

> The prefrontal cortex is the decision-making part of the brain, responsible for your child's ability to plan and think about the consequences of actions, solve problems and control impulses. Changes in this part of the brain continue into early adulthood. Because the prefrontal cortex is still developing, teenagers might rely on a part of the brain called the amygdala to make decisions and solve problems more than adults do. The amygdala is associated with emotions, impulses, aggression and instinctive [behaviour].[1]

As human beings, we are wired for survival, so we use any tools at our disposal to navigate rough terrain. For kids who are trying to figure out the world around them, any perceived threat will place them in a defensive position, whether they act that out or internalize it.

Control parenting might seem to work on the surface, but over time proves to be detrimental to everyone involved. It's the perfect soil for sour emotions to fester and for children who squash their feelings to grow up into people-pleasers who continue to hold everything in.

> Disconnection in children may manifest itself in different ways from outbursts to passiveness, but it always has the same result if not addressed: children who grow into adults without the proper tools to process their feelings, which begins the dysfunctional cycle all over again if they become parents.

I remember asking Pia just a couple of years into my connected parenting journey which punishment she disliked the most, and she responded with "timeout." When I asked her why, she told me she never knew when I was going to come back and "let her out." Thinking about timeouts that way allowed me to really understand what it feels like to be punished and its long-lasting effects. I never wanted my child to feel alone in their wrongdoing again. I have worked hard to make this a reality. I am not always successful, but I try, and my heart feels differently about punishments now.

"Good" vs. "Bad": The Pitfalls of Labeling Our Children

Since we live in a society that values labels, it's no surprise that we label our children, too. It's so easy to put them in a "good" or "bad" category based on how they behave. When kids don't conform to our standards, we label them as disobedient, rebellious, or even difficult. More often than not, when we are challenged by a child, it's easier to label them as a problem child and push them into a corner, rather than consider that something deeper is going on. I learned the hard way that apathy, or "just tolerating" our children's behavior, is not a solution.

Labeling our child as "good" or "bad" is like throwing in the towel. If we're going to label them, I prefer to use the term "human" because ultimately, that's what everything boils down to—our humanity.

We are all constantly in a state of trying to figure out how to navigate life. From childhood to adulthood, the only certainty is that the world continues to change. Our ability to adapt directly correlates to the tools we have on hand and, for our children, their toolbox is limited.

Labels create a false narrative that doesn't take into consideration the ever-evolving relationship that we have with ourselves and the world around us. They're inflexible and shackle the receiver to the lifelong pursuit of either trying to live up to an expectation that they can't deliver or outrunning one that's become a pervasive dark shadow.

Think back to your high school years. If I asked you how you were labeled, it probably wouldn't be a far stretch to come up with the box you were placed in (smart, class clown, deadbeat, jock, geek, popular, etc.). High school can be unwaveringly harsh. Even years later, you could still be affected by the branding.

Now imagine being branded by your parents. If you experienced this as a child, then good or bad, you know labels continue to follow you throughout life, and because they are unforgiving, they roll seamlessly into your lifestyle and rear their heads when you least expect it.

No one wants to live their life with constant reminders of who they "used to be", the mistakes they made, or where they messed up, including our kids. Walking the tightrope of other people's expectations is always a dangerous balancing act because you never know which way the wind will blow.

Think about it. What does "good" child actually mean? Is there a set standard? If so, who defines it, and what's included in the definition? Or does it depend on how *I* choose to define it? And if the definition is based on my opinion, how do we know that my definition isn't biased—some arbitrary rule that I've created in my mind based on my past experiences, society's opinions, or other influences? Also, how can a child live up to the "good" expectation that's homegrown in my head? If they don't meet that expectation, does it strip them of their self-esteem and push them toward pleasing people? Or does it do the opposite, causing them to lash out and push everyone away? Either response is a recipe for disaster.

We all make mistakes, and it's impossible to live up to the perfection society requires to be considered a "good" kid or a "good" parent.

Hard-Won Lessons in Parenting

Pia was great once I started letting her emote, cry and push back. Once I got rid of the punishments, and she saw how I allowed Esme to have her feelings, she eventually felt safe enough to show me, too. She had to size me up first, so it took her some time. She needed to see if I was really going to be there for her or send her away to deal with her upsets.

As soon as she felt safe, she let me have those feelings, all of them. One to two-hour tantrums for a week and then smaller ones for weeks to come. Big ugly things came out, fears of her sleep apnea, fears of sleeping alone because I "made" her. Fears and sadness broke my heart but simultaneously made me realize that the cooperative child is not always the happy one. That just because she could or forced herself to comply didn't mean she wanted to, or that it felt good. Pia was well on her way to being a people pleaser.

What happens to the kids who grow up and all they know how to do is put others' needs before theirs? They grow up unable to find intrinsic happiness. My loving sister runs this way, and it's been a struggle for her to listen to herself, her gut, and her intuition. I worry more about these folks as everything becomes an internal struggle as opposed to our strong-willed ones where the struggle is so obviously outward. At least it gets out. Not necessarily in the best way, but it gets out.

From childhood to adulthood, inconstancy in the life of your child will be the norm. Remember, they're trying to figure everything out, so from one day to the next, it might be a challenge to know which version you're getting.

Children "act out" to get their unmet needs fulfilled. If they feel disrespected, mistreated, unloved, or misunderstood, their behavior will reflect it.

Natural Consequences

Natural consequences are things that occur without our involvement. Sometimes we believe a natural consequence is something that happens after we put a rule in place and our child breaks it. Like, "If you don't take a bath, then we can't read the book." Well, that's not natural, that is adult induced.

We can choose to read the book if we want to even if the bath is not taken, but we are choosing not to because we have imposed a consequence based on their action.

A natural consequence is something that happens naturally. If you leave your jacket on the bus, you may never see your jacket again. That is a natural consequence, and we don't need to add an extra helping of shame onto that natural consequence by giving our child an additional punishment or consequence. They do not help children learn to take responsibility for their actions, only feel bad about them. Making mistakes and feeling the natural shame and upset teaches the lesson.

My daughter Pia is a competitive dancer and loves it! Her self-dedication to this art form is remarkable to see. Before her first competition this year, I asked her if she wanted to work on her solo dance and take a few private classes to get ready for the event. She assured me she didn't need to and that she could practice at home on her own. I checked in again before the competition to see if she'd changed her mind, and she said "no." I didn't push the issue because I thought, *Hey, this is her life and her competition, so it is up to her how she wants to perform.*

On competition day, she didn't perform as well as she'd hoped. Deflated, she didn't talk on the drive home. Once we hit the freeway, huge crocodile tears began to fall. Suddenly she was sobbing, and I knew why. I asked her if she was upset about the competition. She nodded her head and cried even harder. My heart broke into a million pieces. It's one thing to manage our own pain, but seeing our kids hurting is the worst.

I told her I could see how upset she was, then I reached over and grabbed her hand and let her get in a good hard cry. I said little and just tried to stay with her in the moment. Between tears and attempts to catch her breath, she said that she hated her dance because her solo was dumb. I didn't bring up the private lessons I'd offered because she was already living with the consequences of her decision. Pia knew deep inside that she'd been unprepared, and she was mad at herself.

After she calmed down, she told me she was going to practice for an hour a day at home and sign up for more private sessions, and she did exactly that. She worked hard and focused all on her own.

This was a hard lesson for Pia to learn, and unfortunately, she had to learn it the hard way, but she came to her own conclusion about being prepared, and all I had to do was support her. When we allow our children to fail where it is safe, natural consequences can help them learn valuable lessons on their own.

I learned a hard lesson about natural consequences with Esme. In my early parenting days, I shamed her for her behavior and constantly showed her she disappointed me. She quickly became a perfectionist and would not accept her own mistakes. My behavior early on taught her that perfection was the only acceptable standard even though it was unattainable.

What became more confusing for her was my inconsistency. Sometimes I accepted her "unfavorable behavior" as an acceptable mistake, which only made her angry. No matter how many times I told her it was "only a mistake", it only seemed to reinforce her feelings of guilt and shame, which drove her deeper into perfectionism.

One area where I was particularly demanding was when she was unkind to her little sister. Because my sibling relationship was fractured when I was young, I carried that weight into the parenting of my kids. Terrified they would feel animosity towards one another like my sister and I did, my determination to "make" my girls get along meant pointing out all of Esme's wrongdoings when I could have just come with love and affection.

When we give our children room to make mistakes, it assures them they are normal. Conventional parenting says that mistakes should be punished, but why? Does this approach really work? Does the disappointment or disapproval keep them from making other mistakes? No. It only makes them feel poorly about themselves, which keeps them disconnected and throws their thinking brain offline, creating more unloving behavior.

Bring on the mistakes, missteps, and accidents, and let them just be what they are... nothing. Without them, we can't grow and become better versions of ourselves.

Falling and Getting Back Up

Before I started on this parenting "remodel" I would often go to bed crying. It hurt me deeply that when things would go off the rails with my girls, my default was to punish, scold, shame, and belittle them.

The punishing, scolding, and shaming were nothing compared to how I would talk to myself. I would berate myself to the point of debilitation. I told myself I was a failure and that my children would never recover from my poison, so what was the sense in trying to do it right? They would just have to live in a terrible home with a terrible mom and endure years of therapy later to "FIX" it all. It would take days for my self-loathing to subside and then I'd dive right back into my controlling behavior because I could only fake it for so long.

What kind of parent can you be if you don't love yourself? This was the narrative I had to change. Finally, when I began my training to become a certified Hand in Hand instructor in 2014 when the girls were 8 and 5, I could listen to other parents describe their struggles, and I knew I wasn't alone. This turning point allowed me to begin moving forward.

I remember attending my first call with five other moms training to be instructors. I listened as one mom was so refreshingly honest about shaming her son. She knew what she should and shouldn't do, but in the heat of the moment, she couldn't access her thinking brain. She couldn't get to her calm, regulated self.

When she spoke, it could have easily been me saying the same thing. At that moment, I began reframing my self-narrative. I wasn't the monster I told myself I was, and neither was this amazing mom, speaking her truth and being honest with the ways she wanted to do it differently. I had found my people. They weren't pretending it was easy, or that they had it all figured out, but they still worked on doing it better. There was no perfect mom-perfect kid narrative and at that moment after this kind woman shared, I felt like I could breathe. When the kids came home from school that day, I remember feeling lighter, more in control of myself, more confident, and happier.

There was less shame, judgment, and self-loathing, only forgiveness, and that felt like a warm shower. When it was my turn to share, I cried long and hard about all the times I made mistakes. I cried often in that group and those tears helped me receive the empathy I so desperately needed. It became a learning ground for understanding, forgiveness, and empathy, both for our children and for ourselves.

This realization and practice of admitting my transgressions and having others forgive me allowed me to forgive myself, and in the end, allowed me to see how my children's transgressions were so similar to mine. They were not on purpose or premeditated. They were just upsets, off-track behavior, and difficult moments, nothing else. What was happening to me was revolutionary. Letting go of the guilt around not being the "perfect" parent gave me the sense that I didn't need perfect children and that if they had a challenging moment, that's all it was. I didn't need to judge myself, my children, or our behavior.

No one is perfect, and we are going to make a lot of mistakes as parents—even when we know what to do. The idea is to continue to build a framework that will eventually be able to bear the weight of life's unpredictability.

Questions:

1. Who was empathic toward you as a child? What did it feel like to feel empathy? If nobody, what would you have wanted in an empathic adult?

2. What do you want when you are having a hard

moment as an adult?

3. What do you want the people you love the most to provide for you?

4. What does it feel like when you receive this sort of emotional care?

5. What don't you want when you are having a hard emotional time?

---

1. "Brain Development in Pre-teens and Teenagers." Raising Children. April 23, 2021. https://raisingchildren.net.au/pre-teens/development/understanding-your-pre-teen/brain-development-teens

2

Stepping Outside of the Box

"You can fool yourself, you know. You'd think it's impossible, but it turns out it's the easiest thing of all."- Jodi Picoult, *Vanishing Acts*

The reason control parenting doesn't work is simple. Kids don't fit in a box. When we try to put them in one, they punch, rip, poke or tear their way out, and this isn't a temperament thing. Even the "conformist" child will find a way to push back when they are backed up against a wall. While setting expectations is good, trying to force a child to fit into a mold you've created only causes stress, anxiety, and even depression.

Not Just a Parent Problem

One year, Esme had a teacher who used a point reward system. No judgment here. Her teacher was doing what she was taught, which was the same information I was given during my teacher credentialing program. It didn't take long before I saw the effects of this unhealthy behavioral management system in Esme.

Her teacher would hand out tickets for "good" behavior and let the kids buy things with the tickets they'd "earned." This wreaked havoc on her self-esteem. Esme would come home a total mess every day because she didn't know where she fit in. Either she thought her teacher hated her or loved her, depending on how many tickets she got.

Behaving "perfectly" in class became her only focus, so she shoved down her real feelings continuously and spent most of her days completely on edge. After school, she'd come home emotionally exhausted and take out her frustrations on me. It was heart-wrenching to see an 8-year-old so over-controlled and manipulated, scared to be ridiculed for mistakes and overly praised for being "good".

According to Alfie Kohn in his book *Unconditional Parenting: Moving from Rewards and Punishments to Love and Reason,* "positive reinforcement exemplifies the idea of conditional parenting." He goes on to say:

> Think about it: What's the mirror image of love withdrawal—that is, withholding affection when kids do things we don't like? It would have to be giving them affection when they do things we do like: providing it selectively, contingently, often in the explicit hope of reinforcing that behavior. Praise isn't just different from unconditional love; it's the polar opposite. It's a way of saying to children: "You have to jump through my hoops in order for me to express support and delight."

Studies show that when you take away the carrot, the "good" behavior also falls by the wayside. We want our kids to choose the right thing to do, not because they're being manipulated, but because it's what they feel is right at the moment.

On the surface, rewards and punishments feel like they should work. After all, that's what "real" life is about, right? We don't want our kids growing up thinking that how they behave doesn't matter.

The problem comes in when we are the gatekeeper of those rewards and punishments rather than allowing the child to experience consequences naturally.

According to education and parenting author Alfie Kohn, "Studies show that children who are raised with punishments and coercion are highly likely to be aggressive and disruptive with their peers even as young as age 3."

When we punish our kids, we take the focus off of the behavior that we want to change and put it on the punishment instead. This could trigger a new behavior like lying to avoid punishment.

If you've ever increased the punishment because it doesn't seem to be working, trust what it's telling you. Punishments cause disconnection, which is the opposite of what we want to do in connective parenting.

Guiding Behavior Through Empathy

When we open ourselves up to experience or try to feel deeply what our child is feeling, we are using empathy.

Children "act out" to get their unmet needs fulfilled. If they feel disrespected, mistreated, unloved, or misunderstood, their behavior will reflect it. Whatever the reason, empathy can help bridge the gap between the parent and the child.

Understanding what our child is thinking or feeling from one moment to the next is impossible, but empathy allows us to engage with them on their level.

Life is big and scary for a child. (It's big and scary for me as an adult sometimes.) Children need to know that we're in their corner as they attempt to make sense of the world around them.

Empathy creates a "safe space" for them. When they know we are listening to them (even when they don't say anything), we become a solid foundation, a home, and their safety net. When we are as unpredictable and frantic as they are, they have to recalibrate their compass depending on which way the wind is blowing that day.

When school started after Covid, my girls were thrilled. Waking up in the morning was easy, and we quickly fell into our routine. I even had time to have a cup of tea before we left. The girls literally hopped, skipped, and jumped into the car every morning. That lasted all of September. Then the dream ended.

As October rolled in and the crisp air signaled the change of seasons, Pia's unwillingness to go to school returned as well. She would lament and complain about how school was long and hard and had no meaning. She didn't want to go and was adamant about needing to stay home.

I remembered well the challenges of Covid restrictions and lockdowns for my girls, so I was tempted to remind her of what it felt like to be stuck on her computer all day in quarantine, but I didn't. I knew in the back of my head that she needed space to feel heard and that even though she loved being with her friends again and going to school, there were still difficult things that she needed to work out, especially since she had been home for nearly a year and a half.

Loving something and also struggling with it can co-exist, so trying to "talk" our kids out of those hard feelings because we're uncomfortable or don't believe they are valid is more about us, not them. We're not helping them when we judge their responses because their feelings belong to them. They are not ours to judge.

One morning before school, everything blew up—lots of big feelings trying to find a soft place to land. I kept thinking, *"Well, you have to go to school because I have things to do,"* but watching my sweet daughter struggle at that moment, I knew she needed space to lament, be heard, and process those hard feelings that were creeping up. She needed me to be her soft landing, even though we were going to be late. That part I had to let go of.

Pia: I am not going to school, I hate it, and I get too tired, and I am not going.

Me: I know it's really tiring. I see how exhausted you are in the afternoons. I am so sorry.

Pia: You are not sorry, or you would let me stay home.

Me: I am sorry, and I know you are struggling.

Pia: Then let me stay home.

Me: We have to go to school today, love.

Pia: I hate school, and you and I wish I never went to this school anyway. It's so stupid.

Me: I am right here.

Pia: No, you are not, and you don't care.

After our exchange, I stayed quiet and let her take her frustrations out on me. I gave her space to have all of her unfettered feelings. I did not tell her how wrong she was, how sweet her teachers were, or how she loved her friends. I did not tell her she couldn't tell me she hated me or school or correct her words or her feelings. I just listened and agreed and was as supportive and quiet as I could be. I did not leave her alone, and I did not tell her she could stay home. I listened.

Eventually, she said she was ready to go to school, and I drove her in silence. We were only 2 minutes later than normal and she was not late for class.

Had I fought against what she said, reprimanded her actions and statements, what would have happened? How long would it have taken, and how would we both have felt at school drop-off? It can easily spiral into a fight and a contest of wills. I just allowed her to win, win the right to have her hard overwhelming feelings with my kind, loving support.

Don't get me wrong. I was trying hard not to look at the clock, become distracted or worry about being on time because there have been many times when I've rushed through a problem or denied feelings when I knew I shouldn't have. But this time, I did it right. This time, I was able to self-regulate and come with love.

If you live in a state where earthquakes, tornados, or flooding are a reality, whether they happen frequently or infrequently, you learn quickly how to adapt to the warning signs. Whether you brace for impact, take refuge in a basement, or board up the windows and leave town, you know what steps to take to preserve life.

Think of control parenting like an imminent storm that your child has to adapt to. Not only are they dealing with whatever situation is causing them distress, to begin with (first storm), but they also have to contend with a parent who seems determined to make them face their storm without protection (second storm).

They feel helpless and unsafe because they can't control the environment around them, so like the actual storms of life, they either brace themselves for impact, shut down, or lash out. Empathy is the calm to their storm. It doesn't take the uncertainty of life away, but it provides them with something strong and secure (you) to hold on to until it passes.

How to Cultivate Empathy

Empathy begins with listening. You might be saying, "But I already listen to my kids."

Listening is not always easy, especially when tempers are flaring and emotions are high. It takes a certain level of calm and focus to be on the receiving end of someone else's pain and frustrations, especially when the brunt of it is thrown in your direction. Listening well can be a powerful tool to help diffuse situations, but it is not something we are always equipped to do.

Did you know that there's more than one way to listen? There are several types you can use to communicate, depending on the outcome you desire. This could include critical, informational, comprehensive, and many others. For this book, we'll focus on empathetic (therapeutic) listening.

When listening to our children, empathetic listening skills take a step beyond other listening styles by allowing us to place ourselves in our child's shoes to experience their emotions from their perspective.

Here are a few ways to ensure you are using empathy when listening:

- Empathy is a feeling you convey, not words you utter.
- Empathy has no judgment.
- Empathy is listening with understanding.
- Empathy is validating someone's experience.
- Empathy is being in the moment with your child and nowhere else.
- Empathy does not care who is right or what is right, it cares only that your feelings matter right now.
- Empathy is connection—deep, meaningful connection.
- Empathy is saying and conveying, "I will always be here for you at our darkest hour. I will not leave you no matter what, because you and your feelings

matter to me."

The key to listening with empathy is to allow space for all feelings without interruption. Sometimes we won't always know why our child is upset, but we can be good listeners, regardless. What a child is emoting about may not be the actual cause of their upset. Old wounds and unresolved hurts may bubble to the surface when a child is merely denied a cookie. Having empathy in these moments allows our child to heal the bigger, more profound hurts below the surface.

Think about your interactions with your child and ask yourself if you fit into any of these categories.

Their story becomes your story.

How many times, especially with older children, do we have the urge to turn their story into ours? It usually starts with "When I was your age..." followed by eye rolls as our teenager tries to figure out how their story suddenly became all about us.

Giving advice is your default.

Fixing what's broken is just what we do as parents, right? From the time they start walking, we're right there to make sure they don't fall, and if they do, we pick them up and brush them off to make everything better.

It's hard to reign that habit in when the problem is not something that needs to be fixed at that moment. Maybe our child just needs to vent. Coming in to fix our child's feelings tells them those feelings are too big or hard for us, and we don't have space for them.

You're focused on whatever will bring peace the fastest.

This is similar to fixing things. I don't know about you, but I just want peace. I tried to suppress my child's emotions so that everything would be okay. As long as she was quiet and calm, we were good. At the beginning of my parenting journey, I would do anything to make this happen, which was usually less about listening and more about coercion.

You wear your emotions on your sleeves.

When a child screams, hits, or falls on the floor in a full-blown tantrum, it's kind of hard not to take it personally and react emotionally. If you are like me and triggered by certain behaviors that remind you of things that happened in your childhood, then experiencing those things in the present can transport you to that time in your past. It's easy to get stuck in that hole without really listening to what our children are trying to show us through their pain.

You're stifling a yawn.

The reality is that the things that are important to our children may or may not be that important to us. It could be that what they're sharing seems like an easy problem to solve on our end, but they need to process everything by offloading every minute detail. We just want them to finish telling us what happened so that we can hurry and get to the solving part.

You're focused on other things.

The problem with multitasking is that we can only give our full attention to one thing at a time. If we are doing something and trying to listen to our kids at the same time, we will inevitably miss an important detail.

You're a mind reader.

Let's face it. We know our children so well that we can guess what they are going to say before the words pass their lips. While this might be true, it's still not the same as reading their minds. They need the space to complete their own thoughts, and when we try to finish their sentences before they have a chance to own them, we are pushing them back into that little box.

"Active listening is simply the act of listening with intent and strategy"

- Nadia Ibrahim-Taney, coach/lecturer

One key to listening "actively" is allowing yourself to be vulnerable through empathy. When we take the time to imagine what our child is feeling in the moment, we slow down and distractions take a back seat. This allows us to walk with our children instead of running in front of them and demanding that they catch up.

This is why empathy matters. While control parenting escalates emotions and causes greater division, showing empathy creates connection and brings a sense of calm to challenging situations. Even if you're the only calm person in the room, choosing empathy gives you leverage—not as a power move, but as a way of directly influencing whether the confrontation ends positively or negatively.

Conformity is Not the End Goal

Ultimately, we want to give our kids the tools to navigate life in a way that suits their unique disposition. The term "good behavior" shouldn't be synonymous with conforming to an ideal of socially acceptable responses, but when our child learns to manage their emotions in a healthy way that works for them. It's impossible to know what this looks like if we are constantly trying to force them into a mold that doesn't fit how they're wired.

I learned this the hard way. I never thought that raising kids would be easy, but I believed that if I came into it prepared, then everything would work out. All the books I read said if I parented according to this "system" or that ideology, then my child would be well-behaved, happy, and grow into a balanced human being. What I didn't understand was why some methods could have positive results for one child, but be disastrous for another, and even the positive results were only temporary. I tried EVERYTHING, seriously, and nothing would stick.

The problem was that most of these books were based on a set of parameters that didn't take into consideration that every child is not cut from the same cloth—case in point, my Esme and Pia are complete opposites.

Think about it like an exercise program. When they're based on a one-size-fits-all solution, they may work in the short term, but it's the customized plans that are integrated into our lifestyle that provide lasting results.

It's the same with our children. When we don't learn how to build a foundation of good communication first, which includes empathetic listening, nothing that we do to change a behavior is going to work long-term. We must first customize our responses to the child's particular needs in order to see lasting change.

Play and Affection

My supportive coach came to me during one of our first meetings way back in 2012, and she told me I needed to make things in my house more playful.

Wait... I am so sorry... What did you say?... Playful? What do you mean, playful?

She explained how I need to play and lighten the mood when things get hard. In Hand in Hand Parenting, it's called Playlisten.

Lighten the mood?

No, no, no, I don't lighten moods. I cook meals and teach children to read. I make playdates for my kids, so they can play with one another. I don't play! That's not happening. No way!

In my head, a parent's role was not to play with their children but to "care" for them—make meals, drive to classes, walk to school and keep kids safe. Care in my mind was not emotional. Sure, I would be empathic when someone was hurt and kind when they came to me crying about falling or scraping a knee, but emotional care never crossed my mind as something that I needed to "take care of" or could be helped using play.

No adults played with me as a child. I do not have memories of playtime with my parents or grandparents unless it was a card game, which was serious business in my family. I remember being scared to come to the dining room table after family dinners to play very serious games of pinochle or pitch. The rules were explained to me in great detail, and I would be expected to know them and perform at a high level of skill in order to maintain a place at the table. I remember several times crying or feeling ashamed because I made the wrong move and threw the game off. I was certain that this was not the type of play my coach meant.

Since I didn't have a reference point for play, I had to teach myself. Boy, was it hard! It felt so unnatural, like a robot. During "play time", I repeated scripts I was told would work, faking it because I couldn't be authentic.

It felt awkward at first, but over time it began to work. Pillow fights became therapeutic just like I read they would, and hide 'n' seek brought everyone back down to earth after a long day at school. Wrestling was hard but worth it, and the morning playtime of tag became second nature—a way to be brought into deep wells of connection each day.

Once I was proficient at those easier, more mindless games, I turned up my skills a bit and began to intervene with play. Hugs when kids were aggressive and kisses when they were sassy. Turning sibling fights into dance parties and any refusal to get dressed became an amusing skit about me putting their shoes on myself instead of them.

And it worked. I was hooked, and I was GOOD at it. It became my go-to way to connect when moods were irritable; my girls whined or fought. It is by far my favorite tool!

The Playlisten tool my coach introduced me to is gold if you can get yourself to fully believe in it and commit to its use. It turns hard, sticky, and icky situations into ones full of connection, love, and laughter.

Whenever there is a situation where my instinct is to punish, shame, correct, or belittle, my first line of defense is to play:

- I can turn a very hard situation into one full of connection.
- I find the mental fortitude to infuse light into a dark situation rather than punish.
- I rise above the noise and ask my child if they would

like love and affection.

- I offer a fun game or even turn a situation into a joke at my expense, not theirs.

PlayListen might look like this:

My child has said something unkind to me: "Oooooh, looks like someone needs a kiss and hug from mommy."

My children are fighting: I intercede and ask if everyone wants to play a few rounds of hide-n-seek.

My children are complaining that it's not fair that one of them gets to do or get something the other one does not: I say, "What about me? I want a turn! It's not fair. Let me have it!"

My child refuses to put their shoes on: I say, "Let me see that shoe. Can I put that cute little thing on? Give that to me. I want to wear it."

When we can lighten the mood around difficult parenting moments, we change the entire dynamic of the family and increase connection. Connection helps children thrive, think well about themselves, and feel good about us.

Our children can speak to us through play. Through games and through being silly and fun, we can speak right back to them in the same way. We'd probably be better at it if adults would have played with us and given us a model to follow, but this is not always the case. Play bridges the gap in our relationship with our kids by giving us another language to share. It is the gateway to connecting on a deeper level and the backbone of peaceful parenting.

Why Temperament Matters

Children handle emotions differently, and their temperament is one of the biggest influencers. According to HealthyChildren.org:

> The ease with which a child adjusts to his environment is strongly influenced by his temperament—adaptability and emotional style. For the most part, temperament is an innate quality of the child, one with which he is born. It is somewhat modified (particularly in the early years of life) by his experiences and interactions with other people, with his environment, and by his health.[1]

There have been many studies on temperament, but one of the most groundbreaking was *The New York Longitudinal*

Study (NYLS) launched by Alexander Thomas and Stella Chess. Along with additional contributors, they followed 133 test subjects from infancy to adulthood and examined their developmental paths between 1956 and 1988. They concluded that temperament could be divided into nine areas:

- Sensory threshold
- Activity level
- Intensity
- Rhythmicity
- Adaptability
- Mood
- Approach/withdrawal
- Persistence
- Distractibility

Studies like these matter because they show us that there are too many variables at play to label our child as "good" or "bad". Instead of using one-size-fits-all "solutions" (punishments, coercion, rewards, etc.), understanding a child's temperament gives us more insight into how we can better support them. It doesn't change their need for connection, but it does clue us into which approach might be best.

Children "act out" when they want to be heard. Whether a tantrum is normal behavior for them or completely out of character, the root cause is always the same—they want someone to listen to them.

Questions:

1. Do you remember being punished? What happened? How did it feel and what was the outcome?

2. Did you ever receive rewards as a child? What did it feel like when you failed to receive the reward?

---

1. "How to Understand Your Child's Temperament," Healthy Children, 2004, https://www.healthychildren.org/English/ages-stages/gradeschool/Pages/How-to-Understand-Your-Childs-Temperament.aspx.

3

It's Personal

"The past is never where you think you left it."
- Katherine Anne Porter, *essayist*

Like it or not, we learn the most about parenting from our parents, guardians, or whoever raised us. It's one of those never-ending cycles of life that can only be modified but never broken. In the same way I came into parenting kicking and screaming on the coattails of my own parents, my kids will do the same thing, and their kids and so on.

The reality of parenting is that it's hard. Period. It's on-the-job training where the requirements change constantly, and the only tools that we have to begin our parenting journey are the ones that were packed for us and placed on our backs by someone else along the way.

For many of us, this means a mixed bag of trial and error, bundled with a little bit of dysfunction and probably a lot of confusion over how to do the job right. I know this because I've struggled with the complexities of my upbringing and how those experiences (good or bad) always find a way to influence my parenting behavior.

I know my parents did the best job that they could based on how they were raised, and this is not about blame, but it is about the need to evaluate our history, find the holes and patch them up before they cause irreparable damage to future generations. If we don't know where our starting line is, how can we properly run the race?

Before we can *really* know our children (who are a part of us), we have to first know ourselves.

The only way to save our children's children from some of the pain and heartache of our experiences today is to change the way we do things now. Patterns can be broken, but we have to put the hard work in to make it happen. Taking an honest look at where we came from and what tools we have to work with will help us gain perspective so that we can make the best choices possible for ourselves and our children on our parenting journey.

Asking Myself the Tough Questions

Growing up, I often felt alone and misunderstood. I didn't feel loved and my behavior worsened as I dug deeper into the hole that these feelings caused. I grew up in a home where mistakes were not tolerated, so I lied my way around them.

Because I didn't feel seen or heard, I swallowed this deep-seated pain and replaced it with perfectionism. Striving for perfection became my way of getting the attention I craved as an adult. This need to do everything *right* would even follow me into my parenting.

Trying to be perfect was how I pushed down the pain of my past, but how we come to terms with what's behind us looks different for everyone. Striving for perfection and control was a way to avoid the sadness of my childhood, to make sure it never bubbled up in my throat or sting my eyes. I believed that if I could be everything to my children, then I would win the parenting game and produce the most amazing and beautiful family. The only problem is that perfection never came, so I kept looping back, trying to get it right.

I went to therapy for years before having my children, but it wasn't until I had kids that all these things from my past surfaced. Somehow, parenting triggered a visceral response that connected me back to my childhood, and I find the same thing happening with my clients.

When we don't know what to do, we do what we know, and what we know is sometimes so deeply ingrained that it even surprises us when it makes an appearance.

I've tried hard to reprogram my instinct to dive headfirst off the cliff every time my kids defy me, but I have to be honest, yelling to get my point across is very tempting when I'm tired, had a long day, and my patience is wearing thin.

So, despite all those years in therapy before having children, that's not what finally helped me fix my broken relationship with my kids. It's taken years of reading, learning, taking deep breaths, practicing, and screwing up to make progress. I don't know if I will ever completely erase those natural instincts, because most of them didn't show up until my children pushed me to the outer limits of my patience.

Here's the problem: I know what I'm "supposed" to do, but knowing and doing are two different things, especially after years of seeing what "control" parenting looked and felt like as a child. There are still days when my prefrontal cortex goes on vacation and I can no longer think and be calm, but even when that happens, I've learned to push my way through it until I'm back on track.

If You are Not Willing to Change, then Neither Will Your Child

My inner child is always saying, "Me! Me! Me!!! I want to be heard! Do you see me? Don't disrespect me! Don't talk down to me, and don't make me feel dismissed, small and unimportant."

I know this about me only because I have tried hard to figure out what this poor little girl inside needs and is trying to say in her worst moments. She is strong-willed and sensitive, and she has been hurt and forsaken. My folks didn't mean to. They were emotionally abandoned, too, and also endured their own feelings of not being seen and heard. Knowing what they experienced doesn't invalidate my hurt. That is mine, just like they have their own. But, it gives me perspective which helps restore balance in those parenting areas where I am weak because I know the root causes.

When I allow my children's behavior to push my trigger points, I take a pause. I make mental notes and often physical notes. Now, unlike so many years ago, I ask myself, "Why?".

"What am I feeling at this moment, and why?"

"Why am I letting this interaction, this upset, push me to yell (Yes, I still yell sometimes.) or become angry?"

"Why do I need to be angry with my child?"

"What do they have to do with this upset?"

Almost every time it comes back to me not being heard or being treated unkindly and disrespected. Somehow I become that little girl again—trying to be heard and wanting to be talked to with love, kindness, respect and thoughtfulness. The problem is, I am not that little girl. I am an adult, and to expect to have that wound healed through my children is not only impossible but also irresponsible.

It is not my child's job to make me feel better about myself, to make me feel respected and understood. That's my job. I have to heal my wounds, or they will continue to cause distress for my children. In this new paradigm of using connection instead of punishment, we are trying to heal ourselves, but this new paradigm, if it is to work well, needs to be led and curated by adults who can come with complete unconditional love and understanding. THAT, my sweet parents, is SO HARD, but it can be done.

Reparenting your inner child allows you to parent your own children more effectively. Because without reparenting yourself, you could remain that 7-year-old whose needs were never met. When your own 7-year-old is having a difficult moment, you might be triggered to respond from your

7-year-old self. This is a disruptive parenting situation for both you and your child.

Our children not only watch what we do, but they also imitate our behavior. They don't come into the world knowing how to respond "appropriately" to stimuli, so we are their first blueprint. We can't yell, threaten, and manipulate without expecting our children to do the same. Any change that we want to see must begin with us. It's so easy to point a finger at what our child is doing while dismissing how we are influencing their behavior.

Being Honest with Ourselves

Facing imperfections in our character is tough. Who wants to hear that our child's horrendous behavior is rooted in something that we did? I certainly don't, but being honest with ourselves has to come before any of the magic of connective parenting can happen. The deep, difficult work has to be done first. Before we assume our child is inherently flawed in some way, taking inventory of ourselves is necessary, but it's also challenging. Thinking about our past, including how we were raised or things that happened to us that could affect how we parent, is difficult. Sometimes we have to dredge up things we've compartmentalized or tried to forget in order to fix what's broken now.

Truth

When my kids aren't listening to me or are disrespectful, I lose my ever-loving mind. It sends me straight to my childhood, and it's so easy to revert back to that little girl trapped in the corner who comes out swinging. *I'm not a little girl anymore! I have the power! I will not let anyone treat me that way, especially my children! No way!*

But wait... I'm an adult. I don't need to respond to disrespect because I know better. I know they don't mean it, and I know it has nothing to do with me or how they feel about me. It is a symptom of how they are doing, and how they are feeling. This experience and this childhood are theirs, not mine. I don't need to make it about my childhood, about my hurts, and about my triggers. I have had years to get this right, and if I haven't, then I had better get to work!

I keep trying to make little inroads here and there. My upsets are far fewer and my self-awareness has deepened, but it will likely never be perfect, and for me, that's a tough pill to swallow.

We develop coping mechanisms in childhood to navigate our circumstances. Some of us will ignore our feelings, while others of us will lash out. Often it's not until we see how our internal conflicts are affecting others we realize that something needs to change. For many, it shows up when they have children.

When our little humans no longer fit into a nice, neat box we can control, suddenly, our instinct kicks in, and all sorts of junk from our past rises to the surface. Have you ever acted just like one of your parents and thought, "Where did that come from?", especially when you promised yourself that you'd never be like them?

This was one of my biggest struggles when I became a parent. I knew going in that I didn't have the strongest foundation when it came to parenting, but because I'd read all the books, listened to all the experts, and put in the time, I didn't think that my past would rear its ugly head.

Understanding Your Triggers

Before you can understand your triggers, you have to know how to define them. Triggers can be anything from your past (event, memory, etc.) that produces an intense reaction when you are exposed to a similar set of circumstances.

According to Dr. Laura Markham in her article, How to Heal Yourself to Be a Better Role Model for Your Children

> While everyone's core wounds are different, for most of us it comes down to learning how to regulate our own emotions. In other words, fear is what causes control issues. And when we are hurt, or scared, or sad, it's hard to have a positive attitude. In fact, usually, we find those feelings so unbearable that we lash out -- either directly, or in our thoughts.[1]

Once you know your triggers, then working through them to find their root cause becomes easier. Once you know their root cause, you can begin taking the steps to reprogram your behavior.

Reprogramming Behavior

Most of the time we run on autopilot (I know I do.). Our days are full of activity. We know what needs to get done, and from the time our feet touch the floor in the morning, we're off to the races. The thing about those pesky triggers is that they can pop up when we least expect them, so we have to be prepared.

The first step to managing triggers is to change the behavior associated with them by pressing the pause button. You probably didn't know that you had one, right? It's the same one that you use before you cross a street full of traffic, walk into a dark alley by yourself, or sign on the dotted line. It's that built-in caution sign that says "slow down, danger might be ahead".

Think about the negative events in your past (your triggers) as a deep pit full of jagged rocks that could cause a lot of pain if you fell in. Our pause button is like the "Under Construction" sign and caution tape that warns you of the impending danger.

By taking a pause, "time out", a moment to breathe, or whatever you need to do in that moment of upset to regain your equilibrium, do it. There's nothing in a rule book somewhere that says we have to respond to negative stimuli immediately (unless our child is in immediate danger).

For example, say your child yells that they hate you because you won't let them do _______(fill in the blank). If rejection is an emotional trigger for you, hearing your child say that they hate you can bring up old memories of being rejected by a parent or friend growing up. Suddenly, you feel the way you did twenty years ago, and that instinct to protect yourself will kick in, except this time, it's not the parent or childhood friend that hurt you. It's *your* child, but in the moment, your heart can't tell the difference. The lines between the past and present have been blurred, and all you feel is the searing pain.

Pressing the pause button allows us to recenter our focus and bring ourselves back into the present. Then we can rationally deal with what's going on in the moment with empathy and love rather than fear.

When we learn to press "pause" and stop ripping off the caution tape and diving headfirst into the dark pit of our past, we are better able to manage our triggers. They won't disappear, but we learn to have control over our responses instead of letting the pain of our past control us.

Your Past Does Not Determine Your Parenting Success

We can't erase our past. It is what it is and there's nothing we can do to change it, but we can change how we frame our future and the future of our children. Our past is not an indicator of our parenting success, whether we had a good or bad one. What matters most are the choices we make each day. Even small changes add up over time.

Questions:

Have you taken the time to uncover any holes in your history that need to be repaired? If you get angry at your child, ask yourself the following:

- What am I feeling at this moment, and why?

- Why am I letting this interaction, this upset, push me to yell or become angry?

- Why do I need to be angry with my child?

- What do they have to do with this upset?

---

1. Laura Markham, "Https://Www.Ahaparenting.Com/Read/Becoming-a-Better-Role-Model-for-Children," Aha! Parenting, accessed January 1, 2022, https://www.ahaparenting.com/read/becoming-a-better-role-model-for-children.

4

Redefining Parenting through Connection

"Shame, blame, disrespect, betrayal, and the withholding of affection damage the roots from which love grows. Love can only survive these injuries if they are acknowledged, healed and rare." - Brené Brown, *The Gifts of Imperfection*

When I was pregnant with my first baby, I thought I had everything figured out. I'd read the popular parenting books, had all the "necessary" baby thingamabobs, and knew that I was mentally prepared for anything that an innocent and helpless little one could throw my way. Boy, was I wrong!

We can have all the book knowledge in the world, but if we don't know how to synthesize it into a form that we can apply to our own situation, then we are lost. And what happens when the information that we're given is not helpful?

After having my first child Esme, this reality hit me hard! Not only was I missing the physical, mental, and emotional stamina to sustain all the parenting information I'd forced myself to eat, but now, feeling defeated, I fell into a default behavior of manipulating, threatening, and coercing. This continued through the birth of my second child, even into preschool.

When Esme was in kindergarten, I had an elaborate system set up for my girls that penalized them for unapproved behavior. This included "time-outs", taking away TV or playtime, and withholding my love when they misbehaved. I also combined their punishments with a "goodie" box to get what I wanted. I used to say that I wanted to run my home like a classroom with rewards and punishments because in my mind that's what worked.

It did all work, at first, because the threats made the girls comply out of fear while the reward system triggered their need to please me. In the short term, it impressed my circle of friends who thought I was such a wonderful mom, but in the long term, what kind of damage did I inflict? By the end of the year, they wouldn't do anything without a prize or praise. They weren't intrinsically motivated to do the right thing. They relied on my control to tell them how to behave. What was I teaching them? Even when I got what I wanted, there was this underlying feeling that something just wasn't right.

Incentives and punishments made my family crazy. No one had breathing room to make mistakes, even though messing up and learning from the experience is how we grow.

Soon my system backfired as their aggression toward me (that they couldn't express for fear of being punished) turned into sibling rivalry. As they took things out on each other, I learned the hard way that caging a child's emotions and feelings is a temporary fix that only gets bottled up to be released somewhere else.

When I'd finally had enough and acknowledged fully that what I was doing wasn't working, I opened up to changing myself to see positive results.

This is why finding connective parenting was such a game-changer for our family.

The Connective Parenting Movement

So far, I've talked a lot about connective parenting, how amazing it is, and what an eye-opening experience it's been, but what is the story behind it?

Earlier in the book, I shared when I was at one of the lowest points of my parenting journey and literally ready to throw in the towel. At the recommendation of a friend at school, I looked into the Hand in Hand Parenting organization and thought, "What do I have to lose?". I'd already tried everything else and what they were talking about was so counterintuitive to anything I'd ever heard that I tried it.

Hand in Hand Parenting was started in 1989 by Patty Wipfler, a former elementary school teacher, community activist, preschool director, and infant-toddler center director.

The organization supports parents by helping them "learn to build the lasting, close relationships their children need in order to thrive". Using the Parenting through Connection approach, they've been able to give direction to so many families. The curriculum and support that they offer is backed by attachment and brain development research. This deeper insight gives parents a better understanding of how parenting through connection can change the dynamics of the parent-child relationship.

The organization's focus on providing struggling parents with the needed support through education and research won me over. It was never about blame or guilt with them. It was as simple as, "Here are the tools you've been missing. Let's get you on the right track." After seeing the amazing results with my own kids, I couldn't wait to share what I'd learned with other parents.

> **"But every parent I've ever listened to has done their best to love their child. All parents face challenges that they did not bring upon themselves."**
>
> \- Patty Wipfler, *Listen: Five Simple Tools to Meet Your Everyday Parenting Challenges*

Why Connection Matters

Here's what I didn't get at first. So much of parenting is based on emotion and instinct. We go to school for a lot of things, but I've never heard of an advanced degree in parenting, have you? Who knew that the science behind attachment and brain development was a practical skill that we needed to better understand how our kids are wired? I sure didn't, but when I found out? Boy, was that an eye-opener!

Suddenly, what I was seeing play out in front of me wasn't as random as I'd initially thought. And my cringe-worthy reactions? Those weren't random either. The best part of learning all of this was that I had way more control over the outcome than I thought—not "control" over my kids, but better control over how a situation played out, which was a definite win in my book.

The Science Behind Connective Parenting

On the surface, connecting with our children makes sense. It's not always easy to do, but on the most basic level, it feels like the right thing to do. But why? What's the science behind it?

It starts with our brains. We are wired for human connection.

In his book, *Social: Why Our Brains are Wired to Connect*, author Matthew D. Lieberman shares the following:

> The human infant brain is typically only a quarter of its adult size. That means the great majority of the brain's development happens after we are born. It matures as much as is possible in the womb, but this still leaves the lion's share of developmental work to be done after birth. The upside to this state of affairs is that our brains are finished being built while they are immersed in a particular culture, allowing our brains to be fine-tuned to operate in that specific environment.

What our kid's brains receive during the most critical time of development gets hard-wired in. As parents, we have an open window of time where we can help with some of that wiring. Yes, even when they're yelling, holding their breath, hitting, ignoring us, or kicking and screaming on the floor, we still have an opportunity to help form some healthy connections inside those heads.

The prefrontal cortex, the part of our brain responsible for reasoning, doesn't complete development until approximately age 25. This means that from childhood to early adulthood, the brain is still developing. No wonder logic and reasoning don't have legs to stand on with our kids. Their limbic system (emotional center) is on autopilot.

When we use connection instead of reaction, we're offering them a way to walk across that tightrope of uncertainty, knowing that we are right there with them. Connecting through empathy says, "I've got you. I know that this is difficult, but we'll get through it together."

According to a Stanford University study:

> People who feel more connected to others have lower levels of anxiety and depression. Moreover, studies show they also have high-

> er self-esteem, greater empathy for others, are more trusting and cooperative and, as a consequence, others are more open to trusting and cooperating with them. In other words, social connectedness generates a positive feedback loop of social, emotional and physical well-being.[1]

The Counterintuitive Nature of Parenting without Punishments

If you grew up in an environment where punishments, intimidation, and other acts of dominance or control were an everyday occurrence, parenting peacefully will feel unnatural at first. It did for me, and to be honest, after years of practice, it's still not always automatic.

Since our prefrontal cortex is not fully formed until age 25, if the foundation of the reasoning center of our brain was formed during a time of turbulence and unhealthy parenting, then many of the negative things we learned are hardwired into our brains.

According to Srini Pillay, MD, Psychiatrist and Brain Researcher, McKinsey & Co.:

> Past experience shapes present and future behavior. Faced with new situations, our brains will apply rules based on prior events to match the current context. And there's a part of the brain that is to do this. Called the dorsolateral prefrontal cortex (DLPFC) — think of it as the brain's "pattern seeker" — this brain region works hard to find old rules that can be applied to the here and now to circumvent the chore of new learning.[2]

The good news is that despite our upbringing and how our brains were wired, it is still possible to change our behavior.

What Connecting Daily with Our Kids Looks Like

When you're going through a rough patch with your child, try to remember that their developing brains need support. This comes through empathy and showing your child that with you, they are safe. It also means being okay with just listening sometimes and not trying to fix everything. Here are a few other things to keep in mind:

Don't wait for your child to come to you. No matter what their age, seek them out and make connecting with them a priority.

Parenting is only worth it when we make deep connections with our children. Happiness, security, and well-being are often the beautiful result.

As I began going deeper into the connective parenting process, I became hyperaware of my behavior. Things that I'd once glazed over suddenly popped out like a giant neon sign.

One of the most difficult things to face as a parent is when you realize the off-track behavior your child has been displaying is a direct reflection of your own or exacerbated by your response. It's amazing how we can see "glaring flaws" in others, but be almost blind to the ones in ourselves. Coming to this realization broke my heart.

By the time I started the Hand in Hand Parenting program, my oldest daughter Esme had become a nervous, emotional child who was highly affected by her environment and had frequent meltdowns.

My initial thought was that learning a new way to parent would help "fix" her, but as I walked alongside her and focused on what she was going through rather than how

I wanted her to behave, something happened. For the first time, I saw a reflection of myself in her. Her pain was my pain, and her internal struggles were my own. I was looking at a mini version of myself.

Trusting the Process

Mindy and James were referred to me by a former client, and during our first meeting, Mindy cried nearly the entire session. This poor sweet mom of two daughters, ages two and four, was beyond distraught by the constant biting and hitting their older one was doing to their younger one.

Both James and Mindy grew up in conventional homes, where this kind of behavior was not acceptable and where reprimanding and shaming were the only way to get the "behavior" to stop. But their strong-willed oldest was unphased by any correction or punishment. They decided as a last-ditch effort to meet with me one-on-one for two months to see if it would help make things easier at home.

They were both skeptical and thought nothing would stop the biting and hitting. We immediately worked on connection. We let the behavior sit for a moment as we focused on the ideas of Empathy and Special Time, and for the first few weeks, they were worried and even more skeptical as the hitting increased. These sweet folks bravely discontinued the use of threats and bribes and had no other tools up their sleeve. Understandably, they felt lost in a sea of big feelings and aggression.

During their fourth session, they came to our meeting beaming. There had only been one hitting incident that week, and when they combatted it with kisses and hugs, it stopped almost immediately. They were dumbfounded, completely shocked that connection could actually move stubborn aggression from a strong-willed child.

Those two were hooked and made huge strides with their strong child while also giving their youngest a place to have a voice and place in the family, too.

Do as I Say, Not as I Do

When I first became a parent, I could become completely unhinged if anything in my environment shifted, even slightly. Esme exhibited the same behavior and the worst part was that she learned it from me. For years, I'd been trying to pull something out of her I wasn't willing to let go of myself.

I wanted to create an insulated world of well-behaved children that didn't go against the grain, but my kids were giving me exactly what I was giving them—resistance, anger, and defensiveness. Yet, time and time again, I demanded perfect behavior from them.

Before I started the connective parenting process, I became easily offended and agitated when my girls mirrored my behavior. I didn't realize they were just modeling what they saw. Seeing a mini version of yourself acting out your worst parts is a hard pill to swallow.

"It is not fair to ask of others what you are unwilling to do yourself."

-Eleanor Roosevelt

Changing Course

If we are yellers and have never managed to get that under control, it's worse when our children exhibit the same behavior, especially when we point our finger at them and say that they are the ones out of control.

Maybe your natural inclination isn't to yell (like me), yet your child still resorts to yelling or throwing a tantrum. If they are not patterning your behavior, what's happening?

If a child is not doing well, and they are not connected to their caregiver in a way that makes them feel secure, those feelings and attached behaviors will rise to the surface. Some kids will mimic us while others will find a different way to cope. Perhaps it's going into themselves or becoming a people pleaser because they don't want to rock the boat and they are more concerned about our feelings than their own. Whatever their behavior, it results from a deeper unmet need, which often can be remedied with connection, love, and kindness.

We can't force, coerce, manipulate, or scare our children into changing. If we want them to be kind, loving, well-adjusted human beings, we must demonstrate that behavior ourselves. If we are easily thrown off balance, highly affected by our environment, and unable to remain calm when things are difficult, guess what kind of kids we'll have?

When I realized Esme was modeling my behavior, I began taking steps to change it. Now, I try to push pause before I react. This helps me to regulate my emotions and offer level-headedness during times of upheaval, but it's not easy! I still mess up from time to time. At this stage of parenting, I understand that making the effort and making amends matters most. It's always about the process and giving ourselves and our children the space to grow, develop, and mature.

Setting Boundaries and Limits

Connective parenting is often considered a passive approach to child-rearing. The opposing opinion is that raising children with love and connection only is not enough and that punishments are necessary to keep morality in check. This could not be further from the truth.

Connective parenting uses empathy to set boundaries. This allows kids to be upset when things don't go their way but also gives parents the space to set limits with kindness and understanding. Don't want your child to have a cookie? The connective way says, "I can't let you have another cookie, but I understand you are upset about it, and I will stay here with you while you lament."

The difference with conventional parenting is that the limits are usually enforced with punishment and then followed up with more punishments when a child is upset about the limit. This leaves the child feeling like they aren't allowed to be angry when things don't go their way and that somehow their upset is not valid or important. In fact, some parents tell me that their child gets upset *every time* they don't get their way. Well, sure they do, and so do I! Not getting what you want is disappointing. It isn't that you get what you get, and you don't get upset. It's you get what you get, and you get very upset. Then, your mom or dad empathizes with you, and this tells you your feelings are valid, but you still can't have the cookie. It's quite simple, yet we've continued to murky the waters with punishments, yelling, threats, and more.

The limit still stands in connective parenting; however, a child who feels good, is doing well, and uses their brain more because of connection also has an easier time adhering to boundaries and limits. Kids from connected homes, for the most part, want to follow our lead because they trust us to be on their side. Does this mean there won't be pushback? Absolutely not, but there certainly will be less.

I remember seeing huge gains in cooperation even the first week I parented using connection and getting rid of punishments. It was so noticeable, and it felt so good, that it became part of the reason I fell in love with parenting this way. It was such an incredible feeling to have kids who wanted to cooperate on their own without me manipulating them.

Our Kids are Watching Us

With modeling behavior, remember that it's not what we say as much as what we do. Often what we say can escape our child's attention, but their eyes are linked to our actions. When we display a "do as I say, not as I do" behavior, it waters down our authority and diminishes their respect for our role in their lives.

On so many occasions, I asked my daughter to be someone I wasn't. I wanted her to be self-regulated and go with the flow by following all my directives, but I didn't display those same characteristics.

This not only leaves a negative mark on a child's mind, but as an adult, we can attest that the same feelings can follow us into adulthood. I still remember the times when someone close to me told me to act one way while they didn't uphold the same standards for themselves.

We remedy this by first being honest with ourselves. "I will not always get it right". Then we put one foot in front of the other and model behavior that will help our kids and benefit us.

What we show them in our kindness and generosity toward others will help them adapt to an ever-changing social landscape that's always in need of a little extra compassion.

The very best teacher for a child is always a parent who models positive behavior. That relationship will inform all other relationships to follow. On the other hand, modeling unwanted behavior is a child's kryptonite. It robs them of their power by instilling fear, distrust, apathy, and even dominance. It's not about the words that come out of our mouths as much as the actions that we display. We must be who we want our children to imitate.

Connection vs. the "Good Mom"

A genuine struggle that can surface when trying to create deep connections with our children is the surrounding noise. People can be mean and judgemental, especially when they don't understand your process. I struggled with this a lot in the beginning.

I remember one particularly difficult fall afternoon when I took Pia to the local park. I had just begun connective parenting and was working on spending more one-on-one time and trying hard not to punish. After the short drive, I unloaded her from her car seat and could tell she wasn't in the best mood.

I already didn't really want to be there because I didn't like parks. In fact, I found the entire experience dysregulating. The screaming kids, the vastness, and the heat seemed unmanageable, plus playing for me was hard. I wasn't the playful mom. I didn't like playing and before this connective parenting stuff, you would have found me on a park bench watching instead of participating.

We walked in and Pia went to the swings, where she insisted on standing up instead of sitting. She was only four, and I feared she would hurt herself, so I asked her several times to get down, but she refused. A mom from our elementary school approached and looked at me sideways, telling me how dangerous it would be to swing like that. I wanted to tell her, "No duh! I'm trying to get my kid down, but it's hard."

Instead, I froze. I no longer had threats, bribes, or punishments in my arsenal, so I felt helpless. I tried to pick Pia up and set her down on the ground, but she held onto the swing with a death grip. As she screamed for her life, the mom from school just stood there. I could feel her eyes on me.

Her parent bullying put me on edge. Just knowing she was watching the situation unfold kept me from being calm and centered. Since Pia wasn't immediately compliant, I felt an overwhelming amount of shame and embarrassment. Just the thought of her knowing I wasn't a good mom killed me. Again, I had failed to make my kids behave, and failed to meet society's gold standard.

Most of us want to be seen as good parents. We want to appear to have it all together, especially when others are watching, but that creates a conflict when building a strong connection with your child. Sometimes things can get ugly, especially when the process is new, and that "good mom" image can go right out the window.

Thankfully, this is only temporary. As you build stronger connections with your child, and they learn to trust the process, the bigger struggles will lessen. It takes time, but the benefits outweigh the initial discomfort that can come with doing things differently.

I wish I'd known all of this that day at the park. It certainly would have made things easier, but again, parenting is a work in progress. We're always learning, growing, and working to get to the next level.

Questions:

1. Who did you feel "connected" to in your childhood? What did that connection feel like, and how did that person treat you? How did you treat them? What did you feel toward that person and how do you believe they felt toward you?

2. If you had no connected person in childhood, do you have one now? What are your thoughts toward them? What does the connection feel like and how do you behave toward them?

---

1. Emma Seppala, "Connectedness & Health: The Science of Social Connection," Standford Medicine, May 8, 2014, http://ccare.stanford.edu/uncategorized/connectedness-health-the-science-of-social-connection-infographic/.
2. Srini Pillay, "Can You Rewire Brain to Get out of a Rut? (Yes You Can...)," Harvard Health Publishing, March 14, 2018, https://www.health.harvard.edu/blog/rewire-brain-get-out-of-rut-2018030913253.

5

Roadblocks

"Children are not a distraction from more important work. They are the most important work."
– Dr. John Trainer

Help! I'm in the Way!

A cool breeze rustled the colorful leaves in front of Esme's school as I arrived to pick her up one afternoon. The change of season reminded me of a beautiful fall day in Oregon, where I grew up.

I had so many things on my mind that day, slightly distracted as usual. To-do lists were swimming around in my head because being busy was the only way I knew how to function. Even though I'd begun learning how to use connection in my parenting, changing old habits wasn't instantaneous. Keeping up the appearance of a "good mom" was still an issue, which meant that I was more concerned about what other people were thinking than what kind of mom I was being in the moment. Since getting things done and being productive were a large part of what fueled me each day, I wasn't always present with my kids.

Esme walked out of her second-grade classroom with a huge smile on her face and looked up at me. *Be present…be engaged*, I told myself. I could see in her little face that she was happy to see me, so I smiled and gave her a tight hug.

As we walked home, Esme shared with me and her baby sister all the things that happened at school that day. We passed several of our friends and their children on the way up the hill, so we stopped to chat, enjoying the friendly interactions. I loved those moments because they reminded me of what I didn't have as a child, those deeper connections with family and community.

When we got home, I could see that Esme was tired. As she walked in the door, I followed her to the kitchen, asking questions about snacks and giving her orders. *Wash your hands… empty your backpack and lunch box, please. Do you have homework? How much? What should we do first? Don't forget to take your shoes off and put them in the hall. Honey, I asked you to take your lunch box out and throw away your trash.*

I knew Esme was tired, but after getting both kids out of school and then dragging them up the hill, I was exhausted, too.

I continued like a freight train at full speed, barking orders and asking questions. As far as I was concerned, we were all on a tight schedule, so there was no time to waste. In those days, for me, the holy grail of parenting was getting things done.

It's interesting how our minds can twist and justify our behavior in our own eyes until we believe that what we are doing benefits our child when it's actually a coping mechanism for our own issues. I ignored Esme's exhaustion for what I convinced myself was the "greater good"—doing whatever was necessary to embrace perfection.

Even with connection tools in my hands, perfectionism and everything that it encompassed continued to rear its ugly head. Having to let that part of me go was like shedding a coat in the middle of a snowstorm. When the frigid chill of circumstances out of my control blew in, I could put on perfection and zip it up tight to feel safe—even when my Esme didn't have a warm coat of her own.

I remember her looking at me with her big eyes and beginning to whine: *Mommy, I can't do my homework. I don't know how. I hate math. I don't want to do it.* The words grated on me like nails on a chalkboard. I kept thinking to myself that she was just being difficult. I knew she could do the work. She was bright and way too old to need my help.

So, she sat at the big island in the kitchen just staring at her papers while I busied myself. In my world, dinner prep took precedence over anything else because it meant I was being productive.

Again, that "good" parent ideal was still in the driver's seat. I was overly consumed with the idea of healthy meals—things picked from farmer's markets and specialty fish shops. Fresh food was bought the same day it was to be cooked because that's what you were "supposed" to do to be a "good" parent. Anything less than that was sorely lacking.

Even though I had begun connective parenting two years prior, I was still finding my way through the murkiness of intentionality and priorities.

So, as Esme continued to protest and complain, I tried to set a kind, but firm limit. *Esme, Love, you have to do your homework on your own. I am sorry, but mommy needs to cook dinner. Please get started.*

She began to tantrum, and I felt my blood boil. My chest burned, and the anger crept up my neck, ready to light my tongue on fire. The thing I'd been working to bring under control for two years was about to elude me again.

I belittled her: *Esme, I can't believe you cannot do this work on your own. Didn't your teacher teach you these things?*

She responded with a loud and upset, *I don't know! I hate this math!... I hate school..., and I hate you!*

And just like that, we were back to square one, or at least that's how it seemed. The only thing I could do was stay quiet and listen. I knew enough about connection at this point not to argue with her, but honestly, I felt defeated, like I had lost the meaning of connective parenting. I'd been too concerned about tasks getting done instead of the needs of my daughter.

I thought we were making strides toward a more positive and amicable relationship, so how could everything spin on a dime?

My sweet child was so happy a few minutes ago. She came home excited and clearly wanted to share more about her day at school and what she'd accomplished, but I pressured her to do what I wanted to do. I didn't take the time to nurture her needs at that moment because I was too busy being busy.

After her outburst, she began to cry, and even though it felt like what I'd learned and worked so hard to grasp with connective parenting had just walked out and slammed the door, I stayed with her during her upset. I'd learned in connective parenting that you should stay with an upset child no matter what, and if that was all I could do in the moment, I was committed.

This dysfunctional dance played out for several days until listening and watching the scene play out repeatedly drained whatever resolve I had left. Eventually, I shared what was going on with my listening partner from Hand in Hand Parenting. Although we'd never met, it was great to have someone to walk alongside me as we both tried to be more connected parents. I was still working on things I'd learned two years prior in the program, and she was the listening ear I needed for the many times I came up short.

I told Katie that I didn't understand what was going on with Esme. She was so smart, a great reader, and always motivated at school, but as soon as she got home, she would become helpless. I needed her to take more responsibility and do her work on her own. I wanted her to clean up and take care of things. "She's eight." I said, "That's old enough."

It was silent and then Katie said, "Michelle, what was life like for you when you were 8?"

I could feel the sting in my eyes as built-up tears threatened to escape. The realization of what was going on suddenly spilled over, and I couldn't hold back any longer. I wept as my kind listening partner opened up her heart to me and just listened.

I finally regained my composure and told Katie how my parents separated when I was eight. My mom told us on a fall day after picking us up from school. I remember her driving up in her green Honda, and when we got in the car and settled in, she turned to us and said that she and Daddy were going to live in separate houses. Like a snapshot in my mind, I remember the trees were just beginning to turn and a gentle breeze stirred the multi-colored leaves on the ground. Down to the slight chill in the air, it was eerily similar to the day Esme had her first huge upset around her homework.

The year my parents divorced was really difficult for me as I tried to learn how to navigate the back and forth between my mom's and dad's houses. I had to help my sister and make sure we had what we needed at both our parents' houses. As my responsibilities grew and I became less carefree, I grew up quickly. A large chunk of my childhood suddenly evaporated.

Somehow during Esme's outburst, my subconscious mind brought me back to that place, that moment in time. Maybe it was the fall air or our similar ages that kicked up my sour memories and past hurts. Whatever it was, I viewed Esme as more adult than she needed to be because I was reliving my childhood experience through her.

I spent several more meetings with my listening partner mourning the loss of some of my childhood, including my parent's divorce. I also talked to my best friend, who helped me draw the parallel lines between my feelings and my actions. After journaling about my grief, I became more in tune with Esme. I set time aside after school to play and be silly before we started any homework. I also unpacked her lunchbox so she could relax.

The more I relaxed and focused on making sure her cup was filled by connecting, the more she began doing things on her own, and if she got stuck, I helped her. Once I got rid of some of my hurt, I had the space to help her with hers.

The divorce, my sadness about growing up, and my childhood hurt will probably never fully go away, but giving them space to be felt and processed helps me to let them go, little by little. It's a journey that I'll likely be walking for the rest of my life, but one that has helped me be a more engaged mom as I learn to let go and breathe.

Unfortunately, sometimes we are the biggest obstacle to successful parenting because we don't start from a position of vulnerability. When we come from a painful past that includes broken relationships, abuse, or other unhealthy experiences, we build up walls that not only block additional pain from getting in but also keep the good parts of our hearts from coming out. Not that we don't show our kids love, but deep scars can make giving ourselves over completely to the connection process difficult.

I cannot separate myself from my childhood, my parent's divorce, or other life experiences that have pierced me deeply, but I can learn to explore those things in a healthy way so that I can open myself up completely to new experiences. When I can manage negative markers in my life, I give my children a healthy example of how to manage their own challenges.

Connection, Not Perfection

As I've shared so far, the perfection trap has been something that I've had to wrestle with on and off for years. I believe it's one of the biggest hindrances to effective parenting because of the damage it does to us and, inevitably, our family.

Even after incorporating connection into my parenting, there are still times when I berate myself for messing up, forgetting that this is not a sprint but a marathon. I have to continue to remind myself that on this journey, the finish line is not a real thing because as long as we're parents, we'll always be running toward it.

The idea of focusing on connection rather than perfection is that it gives us breathing room to make mistakes and not be so hard on ourselves when we do. This is the hardest part—the mistakes, but they are a reality of parenting and always will be. There's no such thing as a perfect parent or a perfect child. The sooner we can accept this as fact, the easier our journey will be. It doesn't mean the journey will be easy, but it will be easier without the unreasonable expectations that we place on ourselves and our children.

In the Introduction, I said that connective parenting is not a "quick fix" because parenting is forever evolving. There is always the potential threat of something in our past that we haven't dealt with rising to the surface. It's interesting how parenting our children well has a lot more to do with "parenting" ourselves than parenting them. In order to show empathy and unconditional love to our children, we have to show ourselves unconditional love and empathy as well. The healing hands of connection work both ways, but unfortunately, sometimes we're the main obstacle. The good thing is that once we recognize this, we can start healing those broken places so that the road ahead is a lot smoother.

Sibling Rivalry

Sibling relationships are complicated, and what goes on between siblings is impossible for parents to truly understand. How do we process seeing the people we love the most treat each other with unkindness and even aggression? It's hard. Feeling helpless can easily send us into a new level of panic. Combine that with triggered memories of our own sibling issues from childhood, and we have a recipe for disaster.

Esme and Pia began their sibling journey with friction, and when I stepped in to fix things, I was often harsh. I wanted them to have the "right" sibling experience from the beginning, and I would do anything to make sure this happened. This meant that I didn't tolerate unkind words or behavior between the two. Anything that looked like a potential problem would be dealt with swiftly.

Unfortunately, my interventions only made things worse and pushed Esme further into her off-track behaviors. Suddenly, I found myself trying to put out a raging fire that a few minutes before was just a simmer. In time, I discovered that my best parenting tactic would be to remain neutral.

Instead of taking sides and naming a perpetrator and victim, I learned to embrace the role of impartial listener and validator. I'd give them the space to share their version of the story without taking sides or passing judgment. This gave them the freedom to work things out on their own.

Helping our kids rework how they process and respond to negative situations takes time, but the rewards when they "get it" are heartwarming and pleasantly validating. I saw this firsthand several months after I began trying to parent with more connection and empathy. We had our neighbor friends over, and I was in the middle of bringing some snacks out for the kids when Pia began crying uncontrollably because she could not climb up the play structure we had at home. She was frustrated and having a meltdown. Because we were getting used to big feelings, I knew we needed to give Pia space to process whatever was happening with her at that moment. Everyone was acutely aware of her upset, including her big sister. Esme looked at me and then looked at her and quietly came up to me and said, "Mommy, it's okay, I will listen to Pia's big feelings."

I was completely floored. This little girl, all of 7, was understanding what it meant to listen to someone's feelings with empathy, not because I sat down with her and gave her instructions but because I'd started REALLY listening to her feelings. She was modeling the behavior she'd seen in me. She knew exactly what to do and how to do it. She understood the importance of empathy and how to show it to her little sister in her tough moments.

Esme would continue this track with her sister and would always feel so proud of herself afterward. Sometimes Pia would ask for me, and I would oblige, but watching Esme come to her sister's aide after an almost daily battle was refreshing. After months of her hitting, kicking, and pushing daily, seeing her come to her sister's aid with so much love melted my heart.

Being who we want our children to be works. We rarely need to teach or lecture. We just need to show them what it looks like.

Raising two daughters has brought many of my sisterhood experiences to mind. They swirl around in my head from time to time as I watch my girls' relationship develop. It's no surprise that many of the ways I initially interacted with my girls stemmed from some of the hurtful scars I felt in childhood. Memories of the awful fights and unkind words were never far from my thoughts. Deep scars hidden by the overlapping of time still pinched, and I desperately wanted my girls to get along and be friends so they wouldn't have to experience some of the pain I did.

I have an incredible younger sister, but admittedly, our journey to finding a connected and meaningful relationship has been a long one. My sister and I fought a lot growing up and things were not always easy. It wasn't until our late 20s, after lots of individual therapy to heal from our childhood experiences, that we connected on a deeper level.

Once we could move beyond the hurt feelings and misunderstandings, the deep, underlying love that we had for one another helped us to truly see each other. I adore her immensely and have learned much about relationships, vulnerability, empathy, and love from her and our experiences together. Her support over the years has been a comfort to me as I navigate life and its difficult moments.

With negative sibling behavior, it's important to recognize that it's not just about the behavior but something bigger happening below the surface. Their underlying stresses are affecting them and "acting out" is the symptom. If we treat the symptom and not the deeper issue, we will never remedy the root cause. Connection is the only way to unknot unruly behaviors, and why punishments will never work in the long run.

My go-to checklist for managing sibling rivalry looks like this:

1. Intervene at the first sign of upset.

2. Separate if necessary.

3. Comfort when needed.

4. Take a minute to calm down.

5. Ask one child to explain while the others listen.

6. Do not take sides.

7. Ask the second child to explain while everyone else listens.

8. Keep in mind this does not perpetuate fighting.

9. Find the best solution for the situation.

10. Coach them to better communication.

11. No punishments or shame.

12. Remember, the sibling relationship is complicated and ongoing.

We do not know where these upsets all begin and end. Just as my sister and I had to work through our own individual issues before we could truly come together and make amends, treating our children as individuals, rather than a unit, allows us to uncover the true root causes of their behavior and offer them the support they need to heal and move forward.

The Yelling Game

As a parent, I'm inclined to yell. Instinctively, I feel like I'm supposed to make my kids fear me. I know this sounds harsh on the surface, but it's a reality that many of us face. It's what I learned as a child and something I have to push hard against every day. It's like trying to break a vice—the desire is always just one bad day away.

Yelling covers all bases:

- When we yell, we don't have to slow down and think things through, so our behavior at the moment is easy to justify.
- When we yell, we easily tap into feelings of superiority that masquerade as authority. "I'm the adult and you're the child, so what I say is the only thing that matters right now."
- When we yell, we can ignore the root of the problem and focus on our feelings instead.
- When we yell, we can transpose ourselves into the positions of those who yelled at us when we were younger, giving us the ability to "control" what we couldn't when we were a child.

- When we yell, we can out volume our deepest parenting fears that plague us: "I am a failure."

Yelling isn't being out of control as much as it is finding comfort in something that validates our emotions and our fears. It's relying on a party trick that works in the short term but backfires when the truth behind the smoke and mirrors is revealed—we're not perfect.

It's taken me a long time to curb my natural tendency to yell. Without making a conscious choice to quit and walk through the steps toward recovery (like therapy or journaling), I would have continued to perpetuate a negative cycle of behavior that could seep its way into my daughters' parenting choices later in life.

One of the first courses I created was *The Yelling Cure* because I knew I wasn't alone in my battle to maintain control over my emotions with my kids, and I wanted to help other parents like me recalibrate.

When you come from a family of hotheads as I did, you're not just battling what feels instinctive, but you're also trying to stop playing the reminders in your head of where you came from. The shame of feeling like you'll never change can suffocate, and the reminders that it's a part of you only make things worse. Sometimes it can feel like an unwinnable battle, but I am proof that you can overcome the impossible.

Once we rewire our brains and create new neural pathways by modifying our behavior, we'll soon discover that what doesn't feel normal now (not yelling) will soon become normal for us and expected behavior for our children. When we discover ways to remain calm in the moment, build in connection to our parenting to prevent many difficult behaviors, and work on our childhood wounds, we are more able to listen instead of yell. This is the approach I teach in my course: The Yelling Cure.

Encouraging Cooperation

It's the age-old problem: My child won't listen to me and won't do what I tell them, not the first time, the second time, or the 300th time. They refuse to listen and do as I ask.

I get it! I have been there, and in tough moments, I still wonder why it feels like my kids are determined to work against me. Some of it is control, some of it is connection, and some of the lack of connection can be attributed to the control. UGH!

What usually happens is this:

Me: Pia, honey, will you please unload the dishwasher?

Pia: I don't know why I have to unload the dishwasher. Those aren't all my dishes. This isn't fair. I am only unloading my dishes, and that's it.

This is the red flag and an opportunity to do things differently or you can fall for the bait. If you fall for the bait, here is how it will go.

Me: Well, I guess then I don't make dinner for everyone. I will just make it for myself. Aren't you part of this family? Aren't we all supposed to be working together?

Pia: I hate the dishwasher! I did it last time! Esme never does the bottom rack. She never does anything.

Me: Yes, she does. She helps all the time, and I am pretty sure she unloaded the bottom rack last time.

And so the back and forth ensues and eventually ends up as a pile of nothing solved on the floor.

If we flip this scenario and focus on mitigating the situation instead of falling into the emotion of it with the child, here's what can happen even if she is still complaining. Remember, she is already accepting the fact that she has to do it.

Me: I know you hate to unload the dishwasher. It's really no fun.

Pia: No, you don't know because you don't have to do it!

Me: I understand you are upset.

Pia: You don't understand anything.

Me: (I just listen and let her rant.)

These rants can last, and they can go on and on. All I do is stay present, listen, and empathize where I can. When she is done, I ask again if she is ready to unload the dishwasher. Usually, she will do it begrudgingly. If not, I ask her to hang out for a bit, and after she is feeling better, I ask again.

It's possible to encourage cooperation even when a child is determined not to do what you are asking. Whether you are yelling, punishing, or calmly standing your ground, the expected outcome is the same, but only one of these solutions adds peace to your parenting.

When we are resolute in our asking and don't waiver from our expectations, we lay the groundwork for a better outcome. Connective parenting isn't about going soft on our expectations but finding new ways to encourage our children to make positive changes.

Remember that football analogy about parenting that I gave at the beginning? Now, instead of playing in the game, imagine yourself as the coach trying to get your child to the goal line. You have a choice. You can run alongside them down the field encouraging and cheering them on or you can yell and threaten to punish them if they don't get there. Both will probably work in the short term, but which one will have the most positive impact on how your child sees themselves and their abilities in the long run?

The goal line and the rules of the game don't change. As their coach, you are the one variable that can have the most impact on the outcome.

Hitting Bumps in the Road

Being a parent is an amazing experience. Without a doubt, it has simultaneously been one of the most rewarding and frustrating experiences of my life. It's a lot like getting on a roller coaster for the first time. You've seen other people do it, and you're fairly certain that you can handle it, but it's not until you are strapped in and ready to go that you start second-guessing yourself. *Can I really do this? What if it goes too high? What will other people around me think if I scream too loudly?* As you ride the highest of highs and the lowest of lows, at some point you realize that you're really doing it. You're conquering your fears!

In parenting, there will be a lot of highs and lows. This makes the journey interesting... and frustrating.... and sometimes seemingly unbearable, but if you're still putting one foot in front of the other, then that means you're still strapped in, and you're doing it.

Questions:

1. Perfectionism kept me from connecting with my children early on. Describe any personal parenting struggles you have that keep you from connecting with your child on a deeper level.

2. Have you felt pressure to control your child because of societal expectations or that you're not a good parent unless you have a good kid? If so, how has this played out in your parenting?

6

Kids in Turmoil

"It's not our job to toughen our children up to face a cruel and heartless world. It's our job to raise children who will make the world a little less cruel and heartless." – L.R. Knost, *Two Thousand Kisses a Day: Gentle Parenting Through the Ages and Stages*

Our world can be a scary place—make that a very scary place. As adults, often we barely have the tools to navigate the storms and upheavals that come our way. How much more difficult is it for our kids? I've often heard people say that kids don't have a care in the world. Ha! They have every care in the world. They absorb them through us, the environment (social media, school, friends), not to mention those things that spring up inside of them they can't even articulate.

It's easy to think that they don't "get it" because they are young and don't respond to things the way we do, but it's the opposite. Our children absorb the world around them like sponges. Unlike us, they don't have an on-and-off switch that they can use on demand. Once you become an adult, you kind of get how everything works. Kids have to learn their own lessons before they know how to filter what they take in.

Just start with the everyday stuff that they are dealing with and add to it some events of 2020 like Covid-19, Black Lives Matter protests, the Capitol building incident, mask mandates, school closures, vaccines, and just the daily news vomit that seeps into every crack and crevice within their ears' reach. How do we expect them to walk a straight line when, at every turn, the path seems broken? It's not just older kids who are affected. Our little ones may not understand the who, what, and why, but they can feel the tension. They sense the upheaval, and they respond in their own way.

According to the CDC, "Not all children and teens respond to stress in the same way. As parents, we have a unique opportunity to observe and note any change in our children's behavior, especially during times of stress. Some common changes to watch for include:

- Excessive crying or irritation in younger children.

- Returning to behaviors they have outgrown (for example, toileting accidents or bedwetting).
- Excessive worry or sadness.
- Unhealthy eating or sleeping habits.
- Irritability and "acting out" behaviors in teens.
- Poor school performance or avoiding school.
- Difficulties with attention and concentration.
- Avoidance of activities enjoyed in the past.
- Unexplained headaches or body pain.
- Use of alcohol, tobacco, or other drugs.

It's important to always remember that our children's behavior is a symptom of what's going on inside of them. It would be great if they could just tell us what the real problem is, but that's not how things work. They may not know or they may not have the capacity to express it with words.

Think about the times you went through something so painful or confusing that you didn't know what to say. Even if someone asked how they could help, when you're in the thick of things, sometimes the words don't come.

Now, imagine that same level of pain or discomfort in a child who is less equipped to process stimuli. Is it reasonable for us to demand that they handle their situations with a level of maturity that surpasses their experience?

Children can only respond with the tools that they have learned to wield. Requiring anything more of them only pushes them in the wrong direction.

Social Stressors

Anything that threatens the stability of a person's self-esteem falls into the category of social stressors. Think bullying, verbal aggression, life situations like divorce and marriage, or physical challenges like a chronic illness. Social stressors often manifest as anxiety, body-image issues, extreme shyness, and even depression.

Growing up, we didn't have social media, 24-hour news streams, and channels dedicated to every social plight known to man. How do we help our children adapt to a world that's constantly in flux? With the ever-increasing speed limit on the information highway, it's hard not to hear about every global atrocity. It seems like every day there's some big news event being dropped off on our doorstep. Our children are facing a different world—one that can be devastatingly difficult to take in all at once.

Every child is unique in how they respond to external stimuli. For example, my daughters are like night and day. Pia is laid back and more apt to go with the flow. This doesn't mean that things don't bother her. She just has a different way of processing them, and for her, I worry she is suppressing her emotions. Esme tends to have a hair-trigger response to the smallest shifts in the world's equilibrium (like her mom). For both girls, I've learned—and continue to learn—how to respond to their individual needs.

With both Pia and Esme, it's best to give each child the space they need to adjust to what's going on around them and be there to answer questions that come up. I observe their behavior and listen. Some things will pass over their heads without a second thought, while other events will stop them in their tracks and cause them to question everything about life as they know it.

Our job is to be a sounding board and a life preserver if needed. In whatever way they need us at that moment, it's our job as parents to step into the role to provide the support they need. We can only be that helpful confidant if our children trust us. When we parent with connection, we cement ourselves as that safe place.

School Anxieties

The pressure cooker of a school environment is not far from the real-world drama that our children will one day navigate as adults. Even though I cringe when I think of some things that went on during my school years, it's nothing compared to some stories my young daughters share about their own experiences. The resilience needed to function and process so much "noise" vying for their attention is unfathomable.

Let's be honest. I barely made it through some of my school drama by the skin of my teeth. I think we owe our kids an extra dose of empathy and compassion considering the unimaginable pressure that they have to face day-to-day.

Bullying twenty or thirty years ago only faintly resembles what it has morphed into today. It's no longer confined to the halls of their schools or after-school taunting on their way home. It's transformed into some multi-headed beast that even infiltrates the devices our kids have attached to them like a second appendage.

The Media

The same goes for the "perfect", airbrushed images that once only graced the magazine covers on newsstands or the random designer jeans or perfume commercials on TV (way before social media and streaming services). There used to be some distance between you and what the media wanted you to see. Now, the only way NOT to see the "not so subtle" reminders of our broken reality is by closing our eyes because the images are everywhere. Our beautiful children are being bombarded by messages every day from multiple sources, constantly telling them they're not good enough. No wonder our kids need to decompress after school.

Our world today requires a different filter that we often expect our kids to master before they're ready. Connecting with our children and giving them a soft place to land is critical. The world will not give it to them. When we stand in the gap and offer our presence and unconditional acceptance, we help them find their footing in an ever-changing world.

Strategies to Diffuse an Agitated Child

After George Floyd's death and the worldwide Black Lives Matter protests that followed, my oldest daughter Esme had a lot of questions. She'd watch the news daily and then come find me where she'd relay everything that she'd just heard.

Understandably, she was upset, furious even. She couldn't believe what was happening and initially had difficulty processing the events. She needed an ear, my ear. I let her talk it out. I couldn't explain away what was unfolding all around us because what was happening made little sense to me either, and I was also angry. But I've been around long enough to know that our world can be cruel, unfair, and heartbreaking. However, for Esme, this was the first time she'd dealt with something of this magnitude. She had a lot of new feelings to process, so she needed a safe space to unload.

Compared to her younger sister, Pia, who more or less took everything in stride (worldly matters were not necessarily at the forefront of her mind), this was Esme's first brush with one of the harsh realities of our world—racism. I couldn't sugarcoat it, so I didn't. I gave her the space to walk through those hard feelings.

Other ways of helping a child work through feelings of anger include not criticizing or belittling their response, encouraging them to write their feelings (journaling), and respecting their privacy if they need some space.

Choosing Your Words Carefully

Words have power. They can give us wings to soar or they can cut us down and leave scars so deeply embedded that the words still ring in our ears decades after they were spoken.

Think about the harsh words that someone said to you as a child that you still hear today. Maybe you don't repeat them to yourself consciously, but somehow their echoes are not far away. Whether true or untrue, our minds have a way of solidifying them so that they walk alongside us and impact what we do.

Wouldn't it be great if the positive words stuck as well as the negative ones? Choosing our words carefully when speaking to anyone, especially our children, who are still maturing (remember that prefrontal cortex), matters.

We won't always say the right things, but if we can slow down long enough to let our thoughts fully process before they pass through our lips, our kids will be a lot better off in the long run.

When our kids are going through a crisis or facing a situation that they are not equipped to handle, they look to us to help them course-correct. If we mess up, then we mess up. That's just part of the process. In parenting, there will always be a learning curve; but when we actively work on connecting with our kids, it becomes easier to catch any wrong steps in the moment. This allows us to backtrack while the words are still lingering in the air and say, "I'm sorry."

My clients Melissa and David came to me struggling because Melissa's nine-year-old son Abraham from a previous relationship was having a hard time regulating his feelings. Melissa and David were on board with parenting with more calm and kindness, but their son's big feelings were overwhelming for everyone. Since they also had a four-year-old son, they were concerned that the anger and violence of their oldest would transfer to their youngest.

Abraham's outbursts were big, scary, and unpredictable. He would often hit his mom and run around the house, threatening to jump out of the windows on the second story. These sweet parents were at the end of their rope but were willing to try anything to get things on track, including taking a peaceful approach to a turbulent situation.

In our early meetings, they admitted battling feelings of anger and frustration toward their son because his behavior was challenging to manage, so we focused on modifying his behavior through connection—focusing more on empathy and play outside of tantrums rather than intervention during the tantrums.

We worked as a team to infuse more connection into the home and level the playing field of the sibling relationship. As they really poured into Abraham, his tantrums subsided. The yelling marathons where he would say terrible things to his parents and destroy his room slowed, and over time, he became more loving and understanding.

Melissa and David continued to connect and listen to Abraham's huge feelings and stuck it out without resorting to shame or punishment. Every day wasn't perfect, and some were excruciatingly difficult, but they hung in there. In the end, their family was peaceful, their lives were calmer, and they had the relationship they wanted with their sweet son.

Stay with Your Children when They are Having Big Feelings

Big, scary feelings are inevitable, especially when you're growing up. Until you've developed the best tools to help you manage stressful situations, including a fully developed prefrontal cortex, any disruption can have the potential to become a volcanic eruption.

This can be hard to manage as a parent because we feel like we're backed into a corner, stuck somewhere between wanting to fix the problem and wanting to fix our child.

Big emotions that arrive at your doorstep can take many forms, from tantrums and grief to anger and even your child retreating into their own world. One of the greatest lessons I learned from Hand in Hand Parenting is to never leave your child alone when they are having these big feelings.

Staylistening is one tool used that can support the de-escalation of a situation. It is exactly what it suggests—staying and listening. Giving your child the space to work out their emotions while you're present lets them know they are still tethered to something strong, even if they're flailing about.

When you switch to listening mode and provide a connective environment for your child to express themselves in, you give them the safety net they need to work through their big feelings.

Questions:

1. Did you have stressors growing up? What were they and how did they affect you?

2. Do you see stressors in your own child's lives and how do those play out in their behaviors and your interactions?

7

Working with Older Children

"A child seldom needs a good talking to as much as a good listening to." - Robert Brault, writer

I met Anne and Howard for the first time over Zoom. Prior to our first meeting, Anne and I corresponded over email. It was obvious from the beginning that these two parents adored their teenage children, but like many parents, they struggled. Things became especially difficult during COVID, with the biggest change seen in their 16-year-old daughter Analise.

In our first meeting, Anne and Howerd tearfully expressed their worry about Analise. She had all but locked herself in her room, only coming out to eat, and she had little interaction with her family, including her 13-year-old brother Jackson. They felt lost as a family and wanted to fix what was broken.

Initially, they tried using consequences to get her to complete her homework or do her chores, but she completely shut down. They discovered, like so many of us do, that punishments and consequences backfire. It was heart-wrenching to hear their sadness, but I knew there was hope. Where there is love and a willingness to make things better, there's always hope.

We worked diligently on creating connections. After 16 years of parenting one way, they got rid of consequences and punishments, gave both teens more control in their lives, and tried to make sure that each child received equal amounts of attention.

It wasn't easy, and it took every bit of our meetings to see improvement. But we did. Analise began coming out of her room on her own and interacting with the family. She also started interacting with her friends again and even expressed an interest in getting a job.

As I'm writing this book, Esme is 16, and Pia is 13. So, we're currently swimming through the uncharted territory of "teenagerdom". I'll be the first to admit that ages 0-9 can be tough, but the double digits are a completely different ball game.

Anyone who has a teen goes through the growing pains right along with them because the changes in their mood, attitude, and outlook can swing to either side of the pendulum depending on the day. It's a wonder they can stand up straight. They are experiencing so many firsts in new unchartered territories like their sexuality, independence, and social anxiety. Just as the "big scary" world becomes more real to them, they have to learn how to navigate it in a changing body which can cause them to feel out of control.

This "new" way of navigating the world can also add additional pressure to the parent-child dynamic. A lot of the things they are doing aren't necessarily about modeling behavior as much as it is about going against the grain to figure out who they are becoming.

Despite this unpredictability, the same connection that works for them when they're younger is the same connection that will help ground them when they are teenagers.

Don't Let Them Push You Away

Parenting little ones doesn't compare to the upside-down, alternate universe you step into during your child's adolescent years. It's probably as close to an out-of-body experience as you can get without it being the real thing.

In your mind, you know that the person in front of you is the same adorable child that you once cradled in your arms, who depended on you for everything. But somehow, when you blinked, that child was replaced by a stranger that you have to get to know all over again.

Suddenly, everything that they used to find endearing, funny, or great in you is now painfully annoying, and trying to reason with them can be like skating up a hill of rocks on rollerskates.

This isn't everyone's experience, of course, but it's a common one. I can't think of anyone that I know with teenagers who hasn't experienced a personal episode of the Twilight Zone in some shape or form.

During these formative years, they are trying to figure everything out. As they get closer to adulthood, they are in a pressure cooker to find their identity. They struggle between wanting independence while yearning for the connection that we all desire as humans. This internal conflict between independence and connection is an ongoing battle that leads to some really strange parent-child interactions.

Solution? Don't disengage.

It's so tempting to disconnect when someone that you love is being mean, disrespectful, and doing everything they can to push you away. After all, we have feelings, too, and the pain cuts extra deep when it comes from the ones we love.

During these years of stretching, what they're going through is not about us. If we can remember this, take our emotions out of it, and just provide the grounded consistency that they need, they'll find their way back.

Here are some ways that I've been able to keep connection as part of my relationship with my girls as they've gotten older.

- Schedule one-on-one time - Special time isn't just for small kids. My girls still crave one-on-one time with me. It's an opportunity for them to decompress while giving me a chance to be there for them. This can be the best type of connection where I'm not trying to dole out advice or "fix" things. It's simply just being there without judgment.

- Organically place yourself in their lives so that they want you to be there - Support their passions. Go to their games, concerts, and recitals. Find ways to be present in their lives, so that they know you're there, even at a distance.

- Find ways to say "I love you" each day - Saying "I

love you" is as straightforward as you can get, but we all know that it's how we express those words that matter most.

- Get involved in their hobbies or interests - Find out what they are spending their time doing even if it isn't your cup of tea. Ask them about it, listen, and learn.

Beyond "I love you"

Saying "I love you" is one of the most beautiful phrases in the English language, but it can get watered down if not backed up by real action. Over the years, I've found some different ways to share the sentiment with my daughters that go beyond those three little words.

The smallest of gestures can mean the world to our children. They will not always come to us when it's convenient, especially when they're young. It's so easy to continue to type on our laptops while answering their questions or hastily respond as we pass them on our way to do something *important*.

I found that when we pause in those moments and look at them squarely in the eyes with our undivided attention, it fills some of those empty places that desperately need connection.

I love it when people take the time to make eye contact with me so that I know they are listening and that what I have to say matters to them. And if they actually stop what they're doing to give me a few minutes of their time, I'm beyond thrilled.

When we ignore, brush off, or act like our kids are bothering us, they can feel that tension, and they will respond to it negatively. This can manifest in different ways, like them not coming to you when they really need you or the reverse—intentionally disrupting you to get the full attention that they crave.

Beyond making time for my girls, playing games is a great way to connect and get on their level. Anything from a board game to playing kickball, or hanging upside down on a jungle gym, are fun ways to show our kids that we love them. When mommy or daddy do something silly with them, it gives our kids a deeper part of us to hold on to—the child in us that's just like them.

Whether your older child has just hit their double digits or they are learning to master their teenage years, there's usually something that you can do together to make them smile. If they shy away from your suggestions, ask them if they'd be willing to teach you something that they like to do. Even if they don't respond to the invitation, they will always have the memory that you took the time to ask, which carries a lot of weight.

Lecturing Doesn't Work

I touched on it earlier, but there's a reason lecturing our child seems to go into one ear before oozing out of the other one. Since their prefrontal cortex has not fully developed, reasoning with them rarely goes over well. At this age, they still bend toward their emotions and what they want to happen *right now.* Trying to walk them through to a logical conclusion that makes sense to us can cause their eyes to glaze over.

Going for the heart first by connecting with them on an emotional level gives you a better footing when you're trying to support them.

Lecturing is just another form of punishment and ends up being a session of us telling them what they did wrong and them having to apologize or defend themselves. Instead, I like to let those difficult moments pass and only revisit the ones that might be dangerous and then ask probing questions:

- What did you think?
- Were you scared?
- What things are dangerous?
- What can you do to keep yourself safe?

When we tell them we trust them to make good choices, then turn around and lecture them for the decisions they made, we are negating everything we said about trusting them. By asking them the above questions, we put the ball in their court and reinforce that we trust their ability to make the right decision.

The other important thing with teens is to make sure punishments are not part of the equation. When they are on the table, it's more tempting for them to lie and sneak around to do the things they want to do, which can be worse than any punishment. If they are really in trouble, we won't know where to find them or what's going on.

When punishments and disappointment are off the table, our kids tell us more about what's going on in their life because there is no fear of "getting in trouble." Safety is of the utmost importance in all parenting but especially teens. My best friend's mom used to say: *Little kids, little problems. Big kids, big problems.* I think somehow she was right.

Don't Take It Personally

I know. Our children can be really mean when we don't deserve it. We all say things we wish we could take back when we aren't thinking well. Most especially our immature teens, who are just trying to figure things out. It's a lot like muscle memory. Our mouths just open up and speak on their own before we have a chance to clamp them shut.

Since they are thinking more emotionally than logically, saying how they feel in the moment often spills out before they have a chance to fully process their words. Being mean never really makes them feel better or resolves the issue, but at that moment, they think it will.

By not taking their words or behavior personally, we are better able to manage our own emotions and provide the stability that they need in the moment. It does no one any good if both sides are yelling back and forth to see who can do the most damage. Our teens need us to be pillars of strength and love for them during what will be one of their most challenging times in life.

When They Test the Waters

Social pressures become more intense during the teenage years because kids are trying to figure out where they fit in, so they are often more easily influenced. This could lead them to consider or try risky behavior as they test the waters. So what do we do? What can we reasonably monitor and where do we draw our limits?

The most important thing to remember is that if there's no connection, we lose our influence. If they don't feel they can trust us, they won't respect us, and when that position of accountability for them is severed, they'll be more likely to throw caution to the wind.

What has worked for my daughters is giving them limits while also allowing them freedom. For example, with Esme, I respect her space, so I've set limits but also allowed her some wiggle room. For example, her phone stays in my room at night. She can also go out with her friends, but I use the Life 360 tracking app so that I can see where she is at the touch of a button. This was something we decided on as a family, but it was not a "rule."

I require family time on the weekends, and we make sure that Special Time is scheduled each day. I do not pry or give my opinion unless it's a dangerous situation (that's where I use my influence) and everything is okay to talk about.

Our children, especially our teens, will not "follow our lead" if they don't trust us and believe we are on their side. When we parent in a connective way, we gain influence so we can support them when a situation calls for our intervention, or we are concerned about how the world around them might be affecting their emotional or mental well-being. With conventional parenting (punishments), any small influence we have is based on our child not wanting to be in trouble, which is not about their free will or better judgment.

Although it's been scary letting go, I believe that through connection we've developed a mutual respect for one another. I trust Esme, not because she won't make mistakes. We all make mistakes. I trust her because I believe in her and the woman she is becoming.

The adolescent and teen years don't last forever. There's only a short window of time before they are adults and off doing their own thing. Working through the tough spots and rough patches is always worth the effort.

Questions:

1. What was it like as an adolescent or a teen in your home? What do you remember?

2. Where did you struggle and how did you view the adults in your life?

3. What do you want for your own children at these ages?

8

Self-Care

"There is enough time for self-care. There is not enough time to make up for the life you'll miss by not filling yourself up." - Jennifer Williamson, writer

Several years into learning how to parent with more calm and connection, I realized that how interactions played out in my house was directly linked to me. My mood and inability to regulate my emotions affected the temperature in my home. I noticed this when I saw Esme treat her sister the way I treated her. When she was six years old, she would correct and shame her sister in the same way that I had reprimanded her. I tried to correct her, but it only made things worse because the cycle of behavior she adopted started and ended with me.

Only when I presented the best version of myself did the atmosphere shift and the smoke clear. This was the moment I understood that connection always begins with me and what I can control, and if I wanted it to have a fighting chance, I had to do my part.

But how the heck was I supposed to be my best self when I was exhausted? How was I supposed to cook, clean, care for and not emotionally respond to my children's behavior, and still maintain my sanity? This was way too much to ask, especially of a person who wasn't raised with people who modeled this to me or who actively took care of themselves. I didn't even know what it looked like to take care of myself. I had to teach myself how to care for my needs, including the basic things like rest, good food, time away, exercise, and leaning into my triggers deeply so I could unwind them.

Now I check in with myself and note how I am doing. If it's not well, I intentionally focus on lessening the tension of my circumstance by putting on a movie, ordering pizza, letting the house get messy, and the laundry pile up. Whatever I need at the moment is what I do, including exercising or just getting outside to take a hike.

When my kids were little, I hired a little girl across the street to come and play with the girls from time to time. I also enlisted my dad's support to help drive and take care of the kids when he could. I quickly realized that the more I did these things, the more I enjoyed parenting and the easier it became, so I did them with more intention.

When I can't access my good thinking, feel overwhelmed, or think I might say something I'll regret, I walk away to center myself. I also find mantras that help me find balance as well as breathing deeply to slow down my system. Now that I can access these tools, I am more resourced and able to handle my family's needs and give them the best of me.

Why do we run ourselves into the ground before we realize we aren't doing ourselves or anyone else any good? We continue to wear a giant "S" on our chest like we can do it all without giving account to the detrimental effect not taking care of ourselves can have on our mental, physical and emotional well-being. When we feel resentful and depleted, we can't help anyone.

Only when we are at our best can we truly be our best for those we love.

Why Taking Care of Yourself First Matters

Putting ourselves first is not about selfishness. It's about taking the time we need to ensure that we have the fuel to support our family. We can't parent on empty.

Remember the sleep deprivation you experienced with a newborn? Did you ever forget to shower or what day it was? When we are tired, dragging, and barely able to function, it affects those around us. Have you ever noticed how one person's attitude can shift the entire atmosphere of a room? Think of that person you know who's always complaining about something. Kind of brings your mood down when you're around them, right? One apple can definitely spoil it for everyone.

On the other hand, have you ever been around someone whose high-energy or bubbly personality was almost contagious? They make the best coaches and leaders because they can pull people into their "world" almost effortlessly.

How we come to our children affects their mood. As parents, we have a great opportunity to influence our children's emotional states. It was a real shock to realize that my mood was the source of much of the emotional escalation that occurred in our home. If we're not taking care of ourselves, it can cause us to be ill-tempered and not much fun to be around. Our kids feed off of this energy.

When we are positive, patient, quick to listen, and slow to anger, we give our kids positive energy to feed on, helping them downshift if they are having a rough day.

Ask for Help

I'm not sure why, but when I had my first child Esme, I thought I could do it all. I mentioned this earlier, but I literally burned out trying to do everything myself. For me, failure was not an option, and I would forgo my comfort (and health) if that meant that I was a successful mom. On the surface, it may have appeared that I had it all together, but it was a facade. Behind closed doors, I was a mess.

Sad and depressed and going to bed most days crying and confused, I wondered why things were so hard and how I had come to a place that felt so low.

I eventually learned that it's absolutely okay to ask for help. Remember that you don't just wake up one day and have it all together. Parenting requires on-the-job training. Each day brings its own set of unique challenges and going at it alone can cause damage in the long run.

When I became a parent, I was dead set on not repeating the mistakes that my parents made. For me, this meant becoming someone that I wasn't initially prepared to be. There were too many things that I hadn't worked out yet. In my mind, I could just step into the identity of a "perfect parent" without really thinking about the experience, tools, or inner work needed to be successful at it.

When I finally understood that connecting with my children began with me, I started the deeper work of straightening out the maze of walls and roadblocks from my past that kept me from being the best version of myself.

Therapy was already a tool in my self-care basket, but parenting brought out a new set of triggers—things that caused me to react emotionally that I didn't even know were there. Finding the hurt is where everything begins. It's difficult to reopen old wounds, especially if they were never resolved, but it is a cathartic part of the healing process that helps you get closer to a more connected relationship with your child.

Journaling is a tool I've also used to help me with that release. When we journal, we slow down our system, and we think deeply about situations that are hard. We find the why, the how, and the how come, and we don't stop until it makes sense. Each time after becomes easier, more fully expressed, and understood. It becomes less about us and more about our kids. This is an evolved place to be, and I'm not as evolved as I'd like to be, so I'm still working on it.

Here are some questions that I found helpful on my own healing journey. Journaling is the best way for me to collect my thoughts and see any patterns of behavior or triggers that I wouldn't see otherwise.

1. What was the most difficult part of being a child in your own family? How did it feel? Don't write about the "incidents", write about the feelings.

2. How was crying responded to in your own family? How does that feel, looking back on it now?

3. When do you become really angry with your children? Why? What is your reaction? Does it remind you of the way you were treated growing up? Considering this, do you think your children feel the same way? If so, how does that feel to you as a parent?

4. Looking back at your childhood, what did you crave emotionally from a parent? How was your childhood lacking that? What does it look like to you now to be that kind of parent? What things do you do to make sure you are giving your child what you didn't have emotionally?

Asking for support doesn't mean that you are weak or unable to rise to the challenge of parenting. Asking for help means that you want to give your child the best foundation possible, so you are willing to supplement your shortcomings—even if it's just a lack of time—to give your child a better life experience.

Self-Neglect Never Knocks

Neglecting self is not uncommon when you become a parent, especially if you are the primary caretaker. We become so enamored by the needs of this helpless little being that we push our needs behind us without giving it a second thought.

Even when they get older and no longer need our 24-hour care, often the self-neglect has been going on for so long that we continue to ignore our personal needs. *Sure we haven't had a full night's sleep in six months, but that's just a part of good parenting, right? Exercise? I'm too tired to exercise. Healthy eating? Hmm, I don't even remember what I had for dinner last night.*

It's not only important to do the inner work to become a better parent, but it's also critical to meet our current needs in the "now". Being emotionally, mentally, and physically whole is a part of the connective parenting journey. When we feel good inside and out, we are better able to take on the challenges of the day and bring our best selves to our kids instead of the mixed signals we give them when we are struggling to find our footing.

Self-Care Tips

If you've ever experienced burnout, then you know how important taking a break can be. Parenting is an around-the-clock activity that doesn't stop because you've come to the end of the day. How many times have you laid in bed at night unable to rest because your mind is in overdrive?

How do we fit in "me time" when our days are packed with activity? How do we heal ourselves when our kids' needs are top-of-mind?

If I make myself a priority and schedule time for myself just like I do everyone else, then I have more of myself to give. It's when I neglect my health and mental fitness that I fall back into old parenting habits. Rejuvenation is an integral part of a healthy parenting journey. Running on fumes doesn't work, especially since it can negatively affect the well-being of those we love.

We all have different things that we find restorative. Figure out what you need and then don't compromise. Parenting is hard work and takes a lot out of you. Don't skimp on self-care.

Here are some of my favorite self-care go-tos, but yours might be completely different. Start with the small things that you can do daily and then gradually add other things in as you can schedule them.

- Deep breathing. Did you know that when you're under stress, your breathing pattern changes? It becomes more shallow.
- Meditation
- Spending time in nature
- "Me Time"
- Journaling
- Exercise
- Take an electronics break
- Do something you love

Sometimes we are so hard on ourselves that we don't give ourselves the space to be human. This means messing up, not having it all together, and struggling from time to time.

But, when we are proactively seeking opportunities to better ourselves so that we can be better for those around us, then we are making a difference. It may not happen overnight, but taking care of ourselves so that we can be there for others is a game changer. Remember that you are enough!

Questions:

1. Ultimately, what kind of relationship do you want to have with your children?

2. What do you value and what do you want for them as they grow up?

3. How can you get there and what do you want to change in your own parenting to make things easier for yourself and your kids?

9

Conclusion

"I wholeheartedly believe that when we are fully engaged in parenting regardless of how imperfect, vulnerable, and messy it is, we are creating something sacred."- Brene' Brown, author

One afternoon, well before I started parenting without punishment, my mother-in-law came to the house for a visit. Esme and I had had a rough day, and my mother-in-law came in right as things were at a fever pitch. Esme answered the door, and the first thing she said was, "Mommy took my toy."

My mother-in-law responded, "Well, when do you get it back?" To which Esme replied, "I don't know, probably never."

I remember my heart hurt. That interaction physically made my chest hurt and my knees weak. I was mortified and felt like the dirty secret was out of the bag. I was a bully! I took toys from young kids. Who was I, and why would I do such a thing?

Imagine living a life where at any moment your favorite toy could be taken, your free time eliminated, or you could be sent to isolation. How do we suppose that feels, and what does that do to the relationship we share with our children? Who wants to live in a home where the people we depend on and love the most also want to inflict emotional pain on us to get us to behave?

I remember what that felt like as a child, and yet I couldn't keep myself from putting my children through the same trauma until I really looked at my parenting and childhood.

Now imagine the opposite—growing up in a home where you are loved regardless of your mistakes, empathized with when you can't manage your feelings, and corrected for your actions through play. Where would you rather grow up?

At the beginning of my parenting journey, I craved being thought of as a "good" mom and for others to look at me and my children and see a "good" family. For me, this meant well-behaved children who were kind, well-mannered, and respectful. In my mind, not living up to this ideal would have been devastating, and my shame would have eaten me alive. I wanted to be what society expected of me so that I wouldn't be judged and shamed by others.

These thoughts overwhelmed me and caused the shame of my childhood to resurface. I couldn't bear the reflection of my past staring back at me, so I went to great lengths to make sure those feelings stayed hidden, no matter what. This pushed me deeply into negative and counterproductive behaviors like punishments, yelling, and forsaking my own children so we could keep up the appearance of a happy and healthy family.

Ironically, I only ended up exchanging one shame (disappointing the world) for another one—the shame I felt for treating my sweet girls unkindly. The weight of the guilt was unbearable. We were so deeply intertwined in this cycle of dysfunction that I felt helpless and knew something needed to change if we were going to not only survive but thrive as a family.

Society has set us up to believe we are responsible for "making" kids be "good" by forcing them into all the "right" behaviors. It's not our fault we come to parenting in this way... our world has conditioned us to believe that if we do not produce children who do the right thing all the time, then we have failed as parents. It's a heavy weight and an impossible responsibility for us to undertake.

We do ourselves a great disservice if we don't denounce this line of thinking. Rewarding "good" behavior and punishing "bad" in order to meet a societal standard sets us up for failure. Instead, we must forgive ourselves for the negative parenting behaviors we adopted and take the necessary steps to change.

We start by creating a safe place where our children are free to make mistakes, learn from them, and grow. It's all about choosing to embrace a new paradigm. If we don't, what will come of our children? When they become parents, will they do whatever it takes to avoid shame, even jeopardizing their relationship with their kids just to be accepted and seen as a "good" parent? I did.

Perhaps this book and all that it holds can help you move into a world where shame in parenting will cease to exist, where mistakes are easily forgotten and intrinsic motivation takes a front seat over manipulations. Maybe this book can help you find your path, too.

Pace Yourself

Developing a relationship with your child takes time. Parenting requires on-the-job training. Each day you face new challenges where you can either employ previous tools that worked in similar situations or develop a whole new set of skills to help you manage in the moment.

Sometimes you pull out the wrong tools and other times you get it right. It's a lot like building a beautiful home. If you start with the right foundation, have a good plan to follow, use quality materials and hire a builder who is attentive to your needs, then getting the outcome that you desire is almost guaranteed.

In the same way, if you want to build a strong parent-child bond, start with connection first. Build a solid foundation based on the building blocks of empathy, and give yourself and your child the tools to be successful. Practice listening well so you can provide the proper support. Then you will see a positive change in your relationship.

Unfortunately, parenting isn't an exact science, but I've found that when you are consistently making a positive effort to connect with your child, they'll eventually get it and crave that piece of the puzzle that's been missing.

When you're starting out with connective parenting, it's a lot to take in. Believe me, I know! Sometimes there's so much junk that you have to work through to even understand the concept of connective parenting that it may seem like it will never work. It's important to take baby steps when you're starting out. Some concepts may be foreign, so it will take time to figure out how everything works.

The important thing is that you give yourself the space to learn and to mess up. It's equally important to give your child space. This means keeping "forgiveness" in your toolbox as well.

Being willing to forgive yourself and your child every day gives you a chance to start over. This means not punishing yourself, thinking negatively, or beating yourself up when you make a mistake.

Acknowledge. Let go. Apologize and Move Forward.

Self-forgiveness has shifted my perspective and allowed me to show compassion to my daughters. A negative past has a way of suffocating you in the present and keeping you from making smart choices. Who wants to hold on to old stuff for years? I've been there and done that multiple times. It just causes extra headaches in the long run.

Now, negative consequences for behavior are no longer my "go-to" response because what society thinks or tells me about my children doesn't matter. My kids don't need to be perfect or act the right way all the time. I know they are great people, even when they can't do the right thing. I believe in their goodness, just as I believe in the goodness of you and your children, too.

Remember that the parenting journey is not just for your kids. It's for you as well. Parenting a child through the challenges of life teaches us how to become a better human being—the kind that we often encourage our children to be. Kindness, patience, and empathy are all ideals that we hope our children will embody. By becoming what we want them to be, we give them a positive example to model.

> You are exactly where you need to be on this journey. It's a process, sometimes grueling, that requires stamina (mental adaptability) and endurance (the physical ability to stay the course).

We will never be exactly where we want to be at any given

moment because we will make mistakes from time to time, feelings will get hurt, and sometimes the path will seem nearly impossible. Thankfully, there's always a clearing on the other side of whatever the obstacle may be that reminds you of how far you've come.

You are always exactly where you need to be on your journey. Whether you are a new parent or one with years of experience, it's all about using the tools you have at a particular moment to handle whatever you are facing. Even if you don't have everything you need, use what you've got. It's better than doing nothing or throwing in the towel.

Solid effort and dedication to a positive outcome have a lot of weight in a child's eyes. Even in the "mess ups", we are teaching our kids life lessons like how to keep trying when we fail; admitting when we don't have everything figured out; or loving them consistently, even when they are less than kind toward us. Imagine what having these types of life skills will do to help them build character.

Remember, kids model our behavior, and we are the best ones for the job—not because we're perfect or always get it right, but because they are ours and we are theirs.

- Always keep your door open so they can walk through. Sometimes they won't want to, and that's okay.

- Look for the yeses and limit the nos.
- Create more harmony in your home.
- Speak your truth. It's liberating!

The last one is powerful. That's why I'll be the first one to tell you that parenting is hard. That is the absolute truth, and trying to sugarcoat it only feeds the false narrative of "perfect parenting". There's no such thing!

It's only when we speak our truth out loud that we can shake the guilt that attaches itself to us and whispers awful things about our shortcomings. Embrace those weaknesses! When we embrace them, we can work on fixing them. This is a lot better than sweeping them under the rug and pretending they don't exist. That's unhealthy for you, your child, and other parents who are struggling.

It's okay to admit to having bad days as long as you don't dwell on them because trust me, you'll see them again. Rehashing them over and over in your mind only eats away at you and keeps you from moving forward, pushing you into a pattern of repeated behavior.

Admitting that we're broken doesn't mean that we love our kids any less, but it certainly shows them they don't have to be perfect either. If we want them to do life to the best of their abilities and believe they'll improve over time, we have to open up about our struggles. Life may not get any easier, but learning to navigate certain obstacles successfully keeps you moving in the right direction until the next one shows up.

You are not alone in your struggles. Every parent out there has days they feel defeated and alone. I implore you to talk about the time you screamed at your child or the demeaning things you said out of anger and frustration because this is the truth in parenting. Or examine why you speak to yourself so unkindly and try to work on being easy with yourself. If we can bring these things to light and decide we want more, choose to do better, and move away from conventionalities, then we can push toward a new movement.

Parenting is so confounding and tiring, something I didn't truly know until well into the throes of two kids. There are days I don't want to be a mom—days I'd rather run away than deal with my kid's upsets and feelings. I admit those moments to good listeners which helps me let it go, move through it and come back to the mom I want to be—a peaceful, kind, empathetic,\ and nurturing human who chooses peace over punishment, even with my flaws.

So, speak your parenting truth, good, bad and ugly. I want to hear it. We want to hear it, and it matters. It matters to the other parents out there looking to feel normal, and it matters to you because without voicing those stumbles and falls, there is no way to move forward and let them go.

Community Matters (You are Not Alone)

Parenting can be lonely, and if anything can magnify your strengths and shortcomings exponentially, it would be parenting. We plant seeds into our children every day, and good or bad, those seeds take root and grow.

Being in a community of "growers" helps make the journey less intimidating. When you realize that others have either walked your path, are right there with you, or are a few steps behind, you see how supporting one another strengthens you.

Although I'm partial to the Peace and Parenting community, there are so many groups of like-minded parents out there who are helping each other navigate parenthood in all of its many twists and turns.

Teaching Extended Family

Bringing your extended family along on the connective parenting ride can have its own challenges. I touch on this subject briefly in a blog post on my website.

Everyone will not get why you do what you do. Well-meaning family members will point out what you're doing wrong or how they would do things differently, and that's okay. We all have a right to our own opinions. However, this is your child and your family, so ultimately, you have to make the decision that you feel is best for those under *your* care. Sometimes this means you'll have to educate others with love and kindness so that even if they don't agree with your choices, they will learn to respect your decision when they see your commitment.

When Esme was born, my father stepped in to help, which I appreciated so much. Neither one of us knew what we were doing. He took a hard-line, authoritative stance and since I was new to parenting, I modeled my father's example (yes, even as an adult). Later, when I learned about Hand in Hand Parenting and the connective parenting approach, I had to set an example for my father to model.

We made a lot of mistakes in the beginning. It was even contentious from time to time, but we made it through. It just took time, patience, and the willingness to hold on to what I believed in, and it worked for me and my father, who has so graciously embraced the ideas of peaceful parenting. He has worked hard on his reactions and comes to my girls with love and understanding.

Parent Shaming (Ignoring the Haters)

In the first chapter of this book, I talked about my visit to The Grove with Pia as a toddler and her outburst over not being able to go back into the American Girl doll store. The reason the experience is so vivid is not just because it was the first time I connected with my precious little girl on that level. I remember feeling the searing stares of everyone around me as I tried to use what I'd learned about connection to get her calm again.

Now, when I see other parents struggling with their kids in public, my heart bleeds for them. I empathize with their struggles, but the last thing I do is shame them because I know what that feels like.

Parent shaming is real, and it's especially apparent when your child doesn't fit into the well-defined box of good social graces. Connective parenting is not a "quick fix", and this makes the world around us very uncomfortable.

When you are walking your child through an emotional meltdown, it has to be just you and that child. Unless someone is in danger, taking your time to help your child process what's going on around them is the only goal at that moment. Forget the stares, whispers, and unkind words. They don't have to go home with you and your child, so what they are thinking doesn't matter.

Just remember that you are not alone. For every shamer, there are many more parents out there who've been where you are and get the struggle.

A World without Punishments

I call connective parenting a movement because that's exactly what it is. Parents are finally opening up and sharing their struggles. They are being vulnerable and admitting that they need help.

A change will only come when we rip off the bandages and admit that temporary fixes are doing more harm than good. We need long-lasting solutions that are going to help heal our broken relationships with our kids.

I envision a more compassionate world. Part of that vision includes treating our children like human beings and giving them the respect and space that they need to thrive—a world where children are unpunished and deeply understood.

Healthy children are independent thinkers. When we give them the freedom to discover who they are, what they can do, and how they fit into the space around them, they excel. It's when we stifle them through threats and coercion that they mirror the same behavior back to us, or worse, completely disconnect.

Connecting with our kids on the deepest of levels helps them to become unique members of society who are not bound by societal pressures, but released to share their hearts with a world that's in desperate need of healing.

I am deeply grateful for finding this way to "be" with my kids. It has not only changed the dynamic we share, but it has deeply changed me as a person. I am more loving, calmer, connected to my environment, and just happier. I want to engage with the world more completely.

Pia, my glider through life, reminds me that easy isn't always happy and that children like her need as much parenting as those who are fierce. She reminds me of what connection looks like on a cellular level and that each moment counts. Her patience with my ineptness is impressive, and I am profoundly in love with her.

I am also forever grateful for my oldest, Esme. She pushed me fiercely into loving her more, finding out who she really was so I could come into my own as she has hers. This young woman keeps me on my toes, keeps me honest in my practice, and doesn't let me skip a beat. Her love is strong and bottomless, and I love her endlessly.

I have been trying to get her on my podcast for a while now, but she has been hesitant because she doesn't know what we would talk about.

One morning on the way to school, I asked her one last time about coming on my podcast. I mentioned perhaps we could talk about the difference in parenting styles between me and what she sees in her friend's parents. Without skipping a beat, she looked at me very matter-of-factly and said, "You trust me."

I thought she would say I am understanding; I listen, or I help her with her feelings when she is having a hard time. She didn't. She merely said that I trusted her. When I thought about it, she was right. I do trust her. I trust she will try to make good decisions, and I trust that when she doesn't, we will figure it out together. I trust she is thoughtful and safe and knows right from wrong. I also am not foolish enough to think she won't make a poor choice or a mistake, but I am not overcome with worry about it as I see with so many parents and my friends.

That day as we exited the freeway headed toward her school, I asked her if she trusted me, and she said, "Yes I do, mom. I trust you won't get angry with me or punish me if I do something wrong, so I am not scared of you."

At that moment I thought, *Wow, I did it.* I formed a bond with my child that is deep and meaningful and reciprocal. My daughter, who is unpunished, is also moral and kind and knows I believe in her. At that moment, I felt like a success. After many failures and upsets, I think I am finally getting there.

Please know that this journey is never-ending. I still mess up, say and do things I don't want to, and make massive mistakes, but I do not stop and you shouldn't either. We are changing an entire society, a generation, and the tenets of our own families. We should not give up until all children feel seen, heard, understood, and parenting is given its rightful respect.

I hope if nothing else, this book has given you the courage to parent without punishments and embrace the ideas of connection while also denouncing perfection and good vs. evil.

Acknowledgments

I want to acknowledge all the parents who have allowed me into their worlds—my clients, online students, and countless online community members. I feel so lucky to walk alongside you. It has given me the most insight into myself and my own children. Every experience with a parent teaches me something new, and I appreciate the reminder of how beautiful and colorful parenting can be in this modern world.

Thank you to publishing consultant Shannon Clark and Book Formula Publishing for your publishing direction and editing support.

About Author

Michelle Kenney, M.Ed. has helped thousands of parents stop using punishments and yelling and learn kind limits to connect more deeply with their children. A former yeller, recovering perfectionist, and reformed control freak, Michelle guides parents in creating a more calm and peaceful home in a modern, demanding, and hectic world. She's worked with children and families for almost three decades, formerly as a public school teacher and counselor and Adjunct Professor in the Department of Education teaching Credentialing Programs. In 2015, she became trained in Hand in Hand Parenting and founded Peace and Parenting to share her methodologies with parents all over the world. Michelle is a frequent speaker on ABC, NBC, Fox, and other news outlets, and her podcast and social media channels have a large and devoted following. She lives in Los Angeles in a peaceful home with her two teenage daughters.

Printed in the USA
CPSIA information can be obtained
at www.ICGtesting.com
LVHW020252240824
788989LV00006B/1151

9 780578 281582